NUMBER 104

Yale French Studies

Encounters with Levinas

Yale French Studies

Thomas Trezise, *Special editor for this issue*
Alyson Waters, *Managing editor*
Editorial board: Edwin Duval (Chair), Joseph Acquisto,
  Ora Avni, R. Howard Bloch, Peter Brooks, Mark
  Burde, Brooke Donaldson, Thomas Kavanagh,
  Christopher L. Miller, Donia Mounsef, Susan Weiner
Editorial assistant: Joseph Mai
Editorial office: 82-90 Wall Street, Room 308
Mailing address: P.O. Box 208251, New Haven,
  Connecticut 06520-8251
Sales and subscription office:
Yale University Press, P.O. Box 209040
New Haven, Connecticut 06520-9040
Published twice annually by Yale University Press

Designed by James J. Johnson and set in Trump
  Medieval Roman by The Composing Room of
  Michigan, Inc. Printed in the United States of
  America by the Vail-Ballou Press, Binghamton, N.Y.

ISSN 044-0078
ISBN for this issue 0-300-10216-X

**THE UNIVERSITY OF LIVERPOOL
SYDNEY JONES LIBRARY**

Please return or renew, on or before the last date below. A fine is payable on late returned items. Items may be recalled after one week for the use of another reader. Items may be renewed by telephone:- 0151 794 - 2678.

For conditions of borrowing, see Library Regulations

THOMAS TREZISE

Editor's Preface

Emmanuel Levinas first became the focus of widespread scholarly attention in the late sixties and early seventies, and it is safe to say that the relative neglect he suffered before then has since been more than counterbalanced by the extraordinary number of publications devoted to his thought. Both a practitioner and a critic of phenomenology who argued in favor of ethics rather than ontology as first philosophy, Levinas produced a very considerable body of philosophical work, including most notably *Totality and Infinity* (1961) and *Otherwise than Being* (1974), as well as a series of texts devoted specifically to Judaism. Yet Levinas would not have achieved his current status and influence were it not that the ethical relation to "the other," to which he ascribes preeminence in his philosophy of subjectivity, continues to raise more questions than it answers, and does so within quite different orders of intellectual inquiry.

It is with this in mind that the Levinasian motif of the "encounter" with the other was chosen to serve as a principle both of unity and of diversity for the present volume. In Levinas's work, ontology yields to ethics when I encounter an other who is not simply another me—an other variously thematized as "the widow and the orphan," the weak, the poor, the stranger, but also the neighbor—and whose very otherness commands me to assume a responsibility beyond the care of my own self-preservation in being. While my response to the interpellation of the other constitutes, in Levinas's view, my own ethical identity, the challenge remains for me to respect as such the very alterity that produced the response itself. As I have suggested, however, the ethical relation that emerges or reemerges from the encounter with the other can be approached in a number of ways. One can ask, for example, whether it is possible to speak of the other "as such" in the language of philos-

YFS 104, *Encounters with Levinas,* ed. Thomas Trezise, © 2004 by Yale University.

ophy, when this language relies so thoroughly on the identifying and universalizing power of the concept. Might it not be the case that Levinas's own exclusive predilection for philosophical discourse leads him to essentialize the very other whose singularity he claims to champion? And does the concern for the other not suggest that the discourse pertaining to it should be other than philosophical—that the encounter requires the intervention of idioms heterogeneous to that of philosophy, such as those of history and of literature? Moreover, how can one reconcile the purely dyadic encounter of self and other with considerations based on the "third person" or community, such as justice and politics? Finally, one can ask whether the radicality and originality so often attributed to Levinas do not derive at least in part from other thinkers he himself encountered, and whether, more specifically, his ahistorical or transcendental conception of the ethical relation did not evolve from his familiarity with currents immanent to certain intellectual *milieux*, even from longstanding religious, philosophical, or simply cultural traditions. Needless to say, any such questions asked *of* Levinas or his work will also constitute, as here, encounters *with* Levinas himself.

As the special editor for this volume, I have had the pleasure of witnessing how, in ways I could not entirely foresee, the seven authors included here have succeeded not only in shedding light on the notion of encounter but also, to varying degrees, in articulating individual encounters both attentive to and critical of Levinas. I have also had the pleasure of seeing how, amongst themselves, these essays have produced encounters at once unanticipated and illuminating. In her essay, Leora Batnitzky challenges the postmodernist infatuation with the apparent undoing of the traditional subject in Levinas's ethical relation by reminding us that the assumption of responsibility draws on the resources of a modern conception of subjectivity originating in Descartes. She also argues against the not uncommon but certainly unexamined assumption that Levinas himself is not particularly concerned with philosophical argumentation. Samuel Moyn focuses on the widely neglected evolution of Levinas within the context of interwar intellectual history, showing the extent to which Levinas is indebted, in his own repudiation of history, to historical developments, in particular the Kierkegaard enthusiasm in France. Alain Toumayan takes the trouble to examine the connection between Levinas and Dostoevsky beyond the propensity of Levinas and his critics merely to cite Dostoevsky as the illustration of a philosophical principle. Luce Irigaray "returns" to Levinas, not only in order to correct the impression that she belongs to his philosophical lineage, but also to show how Levinas, while perhaps unusual among his contemporaries in his thinking about sexuality, nevertheless remains imprisoned in a masculine sameness when trying precisely to articulate the alterity of the feminine. Paul Ricoeur proposes a concentrated reading of *Otherwise than Being* in order to ask previously unasked or deliberately ignored questions pertaining in particular to the troubling claim that it is the violent, traumatizing force of the encounter that produces goodness and to the bewildering contradiction between Levinas's systematic dismissal of memory as a vehicle of assimilation and his clear devotion to the memory of those, including his own family, who perished in the Holocaust. Philippe Crignon examines at length the development and tensions in Levinas's reflections on figuration, showing how, with respect both to sexuality and to art, Levinas's explicit positions are at odds with what his philosophy of subjectivity enables us to think about these. Finally, Edith Wyschogrod moves Levinas studies into a new area by staging a confrontation between Levinas's understanding of alterity and recent developments in genetic theory.

Works by Emmanuel Levinas Cited

Listed below are the works by Emmanuel Levinas quoted in this issue, preceded by the abbreviations used for page references. References are made only to the English translations of Levinas. Where such translations have appeared only in collections, we cite, below, the English text alone. For the sake of faithfulness to the original French and reasonable consistency, however, published translations have frequently been modified by the authors, the translators, or the editor.

[AT] *Alterity and Transcendence*. Translated by Michael B. Smith. New York: Columbia University Press, 1999. Originally published as *Altérité et transcendance*. Montpellier: Fata Morgana, 1995.

[BPW] *Basic Philosophical Writings*. Edited by Adriaan T. Peperzak, Simon Critchley, and Robert Bernasconi. Bloomington: Indiana University Press, 1996.

[CPP] *Collected Philosophical Papers*. Translated by Alphonso Lingis. Dordrecht: Martinus Nijhoff, 1987.

[DC] *Deconstruction in Context* ["The Trace of the Other"]. Edited by Mark C. Taylor. Chicago: University of Chicago Press, 1986.

[DF] *Difficult Freedom: Essays on Judaism*. Translated by Seán Hand. Baltimore: The Johns Hopkins University Press, 1990. Originally published as *Difficile liberté: Essais sur le judaïsme*. Paris: Albin Michel, 1976 [1963].

[EI] *Ethics and Infinity: Conversations with Philippe Nemo*. Translated by Richard A. Cohen. Pittsburgh: Duquesne University Press, 1985. Originally published as *Éthique et infini*. Paris: Fayard, 1982.

[EN] *Entre Nous: Thinking-Of-The-Other*. Translated by Michael B.

YFS 104, *Encounters with Levinas*, ed. Thomas Trezise, © 2004 by Yale University.

4

Smith and Barbara Harshav. New York: Columbia University Press, 1998. Originally published as *Entre nous: Essais sur le penser-à-l'autre*. Paris: Grasset, 1991.

[*GDT*]   *God, Death, and Time*. Translated by Bettina Bergo. Stanford: Stanford University Press, 2000. Originally published as *Dieu, la mort et le temps*. Paris: Grasset, 1993.

[*OB*]   *Otherwise than Being or Beyond Essence*. Translated by Alphonso Lingis. The Hague: Martinus Nijhoff, 1981; Pittsburgh: Duquesne University Press, 1998. Originally published as *Autrement qu'être ou au-delà de l'essence*. The Hague: Martinus Nijhoff, 1974.

[*OG*]   *Of God Who Comes to Mind*. Translated by Bettina Bergo. Stanford: Stanford University Press, 1998. Originally published as *De Dieu qui vient à l'idée*. Paris: Vrin, 1982.

[*PN*]   *Proper Names*. Translated by Michael B. Smith. Stanford: Stanford University Press, 1996. Originally published as *Noms propres*. Montpellier: Fata Morgana, 1976.

[*TI*]   *Totality and Infinity: An Essay on Exteriority*. Translated by Alphonso Lingis. Pittsburgh: Duquesne University Press, 1969. Originally published as *Totalité et infini: Essai sur l'extériorité*. The Hague: Martinus Nijhoff, 1961.

[*TO*]   *Time and the Other*. Translated by Richard A. Cohen. Pittsburgh: Duquesne University Press, 1987. Originally published as *Le temps et l'autre*. Montpellier: Fata Morgana, 1979.

LEORA BATNITZKY

Encountering the Modern Subject in Levinas

INTRODUCTION

The scholarly literature on Levinas and Descartes is surprisingly sparse, given Levinas's bold claims in *Totality and Infinity* that he is drawing on a number of profound Cartesian insights. Some attention has been given to Levinas's use of Descartes's conception of infinity and some to his use of Descartes's evil genius in arguing for a goodness beyond being.[1] My focus in this essay, however, is on Levinas's appropriation of Descartes's philosophy in order to argue for a separable, independent subject. Levinas's claim about ethics rests upon his elucidation of the subject of ethics, the "I" who is uniquely responsible. It is the separate, independent, indeed atheistic self that he means to affirm in *Totality and Infinity*. Despite his arguments about the inability of philosophy to grasp the face of the other, Levinas's project is nothing short of a defense of the modern philosophical project—and the modern subject in particular—after Heidegger.

If postmodern philosophy takes as its villain the subject of Descartes's *cogito,* the reading of Levinas presented in this essay calls into question the view of Levinas as a "postmodern" thinker. I argue in what follows that Levinas's phenomenological description of the subject in *Totality and Infinity*, and also in *Otherwise than Being*, bears its greatest debt to Descartes. Levinas in fact presents his readers with an ethical encounter with Descartes's modern subject—an encounter that he claims is already present in Descartes.

Yet surely, one would quickly reply, Levinas's subject is not Des-

---

1. Of particular interest is Robert Bernasconi's "The Silent Anarchic World of the Evil Genius," in G. Moneta, J. Sallis, and J. Taminiaux, eds., *The Collegium Phaenomenologicum: The First Ten Years* (Dordrecht: Kluwer, 1988), 257–72.

YFS 104, *Encounters with Levinas,* ed. Thomas Trezise, © 2004 by Yale University.

cartes's subject. I argue in what follows, however, that the subject described by *Totality and Infinity* is none other than Descartes's so-called modern subject. In an important sense, this claim isn't even a claim because Levinas says as much. If Heidegger, in *Being and Time*, takes Descartes to have expressed and determined the modern dichotomy between subject and object, Levinas seeks nothing less than to reaffirm such a distinction. In order to appreciate Levinas's arguments, as well as their impetus, we must turn to his debt to and reliance on Husserl's view of the ego. To be sure, Levinas transforms Husserl's egology into an ethics of the other. Yet against Heidegger, he turns to Husserl's account of the ego to offer his view of ethics. We will see, however, that in returning to Husserl, Levinas in fact returns (as he himself says) to Descartes. Where Husserl locates Descartes's mistake in the claim that the ego is "a piece of the world,"[2] Levinas reaffirms, against Husserl, Descartes's initial impulse. In order to appreciate this appropriation of Descartes, we turn now to the overall argument of Levinas's first major philosophical work, *Totality and Infinity*.

PART ONE: THE ARGUMENT OF *TOTALITY AND INFINITY*

Totality and Infinity does not make a linear argument. Levinas seems to move from claim to claim without any apparent attempt to alert his readers to a clear progression of thought. A number of interpreters have commented that this lack of linear argument is part and parcel of his philosophical claim that ethics is first philosophy. These interpreters contend that Levinas's claims about ethics do not lend themselves to propositional argument. Yet while there is certainly much to be said about Levinas's style and choice of structure, *Totality and Infinity* does make a philosophical argument, one that we can outline fairly clearly. I make this claim for two reasons. First, this view conforms to Levinas's own self-understanding. Levinas very much understands himself as a philosopher in the phenomenological tradition. As such, he must have an argument to present that can be questioned, for this is the business of philosophy. Second, by appreciating the actual argument of *Totality and Infinity*, we can grasp Levinas's central *philosophical* claim, which is not, as many might believe, a claim about the self's obligation to the other. While this contention of course marks Levinas's entire philo-

2. Edmund Husserl, *Cartesian Meditations,* trans. Dorion Cairns (The Hague: Martinus Nijhoff, 1960), 26.

sophical project, his central argument in *Totality and Infinity* is for a separable, independent subject. If Levinas can adequately describe and argue for such a subject, then his claim about ethics follows.

I have set myself the not small task, then, of explaining the structure of *Totality and Infinity*. For despite the book's complexity, there is a structure to it and its argument emerges from this structure. To appreciate this, we must turn to the table of contents, which I reproduce here:

In Section I, "The Same and the Other," Levinas lays out what will be the argument, to be made in greater detail, in the next three sections. Section I itself has four parts, which mirror the structure of the book as a whole. Part A of Section I, "Metaphysics and Transcendence," de-

scribes the broad arguments that are developed in the next three parts
(B–D). In this part, Levinas lays out his general claim: that ethics precedes ontology and that ethics is transcendence. The following three
parts (B–D) make in short the argument that Levinas will make in the
second through fourth sections of the book. Part B, "Separation and
Discourse," makes in short the argument of Section II, "Interiority and
Economy." Part C, "Truth and Justice," makes the argument that Section III of the book, "Exteriority and the Face," will make in greater detail. And Part D, "Separation and the Absolute," introduces the argument that will be made in Section IV, "Beyond the Face."

What then is the argument? As is well known, Levinas contends
that ethics is first philosophy. My obligation to another person, Levinas claims, logically precedes anything that we can say about the nature of being. The most fundamental fact of my humanity concerns
this obligation I have to another person. Levinas means to upset the
equation between self and other, politics and ethics, and indeed between totality and infinity. By virtue of its own language, it is possible
to read *Totality and Infinity* as establishing these dichotomies. Yet Levinas's philosophical goal is much more complex. He intends to show
not that there is a dichotomy between self and other, politics and
ethics, or totality and infinity, but rather that the latter term in each of
these pairs makes possible the former term, without subsuming the reality of the former term into itself. In the case of self and other, this
means that Levinas argues not for altruism, which would be the view
of ethics based on a dichotomy between self and other, but for an ethics
of infinite responsibility that makes truly independent selves possible.
But these arguments, along with Levinas's radical claim about ethics,
grow out of his initial contention concerning the separable self. Indeed,
Levinas's entire argument in *Totality and Infinity* hangs on his con-
tentions about a truly separable, independent self.

Before turning to the specifics of Levinas's arguments, let us look
once again at the structure of *Totality and Infinity*. Levinas's broad
claims are reflected, respectively, by the four parts of Section I in their
first subtitle. The subtitle of Part A is "Desire for the Invisible." Ethics
for Levinas is the movement beyond the visible. The face of the other,
which would seem to imply visuality, is in fact for Levinas not grasp-
able by vision or thought. Desire for the invisible is, for him, desire for
infinity. However, the desire for the invisible can only happen within
the visible. Hence an account of the invisible requires an account of the
visible. An account of infinity requires an account of totality. If the de-

sire for the invisible is the task of ethics (and Levinas begins his study by stating that it is), then he must first provide an account of the visible. This is the goal of parts B–D of Section I. And again, these parts mirror the more detailed arguments Levinas makes in Sections II–IV. To appreciate the abbreviated arguments of Parts B–D of Section I, we must, as I've suggested, take their first subtitles into account. In Part B, the first subtitle is "Atheism or the Will"; in Part C, it is "Freedom Called into Question"; and in Part D, which is not subdivided, we will consider it to be "Separation and the Absolute."

Simply put, the argument of *Totality and Infinity* is as follows. If we desire the invisible (which Levinas defines as the ethical stance), then we must recognize what is necessary to make this desire itself possible. The first and, I will argue, most important element in Levinas's argument pertains to "atheism or the will." In the detailed phenomenological descriptions of Section II of *Totality and Infinity* (entitled "Interiority and Economy"), Levinas sketches a picture of the atheistic self. If this sketch is successful, then his phenomenological descriptions in Section III (entitled "Exteriority and the Face") follow from it. In other words, Levinas's arguments about my obligation to another depend philosophically upon whether he can successfully describe the atheistic self.

Section IV of *Totality and Infinity*, entitled "Beyond the Face," is Levinas's attempt to bring his analysis of the self and the other, of the worlds of totality and infinity, into phenomenological relation with his descriptions of the world of social relations, defined here for him primarily by the relations of the family. Returning to the title of Section I Part D, "Separation and the Absolute," it becomes clear that Levinas's attempt in Section IV is to describe the ways in which separate beings come together to create the ethical relation, which is for Levinas "the absolute." But Levinas's ethical relation is not (in this sense at least) Buber's dialogical encounter. Two separate beings, male and female, come together for Levinas not to encounter one another ethically but to create the ethical relationship between parent and child (what Levinas calls father and son). Here we find the argument of Sections II and III repeated in new form: separation is necessary for a glimpse (not visual of course) of the absoluteness of the ethical relation. In the conclusion of *Totality and Infinity*, Levinas considers the implications of his view of separation and the absolute for the concepts of religion and politics, themes he continues to develop throughout his later work.

While there is of course much more to be said about the structure and argument of *Totality and Infinity*, what I would like to make clear is that the central argument of this work is for the separable self. Levinas's radical claim about ethics rests neither on a philosophical argument for altruism nor even on a philosophical argument for ethics per se. Rather, I suggest that the philosophical claims of *Totality and Infinity* rest upon Levinas's attempt to affirm phenomenologically a picture of an independent, isolated subject.

PART II: HEIDEGGER AND HUSSERL

In order to appreciate Levinas's arguments about the self, we must discuss briefly Husserl's and Heidegger's respective views of the self. In affirming an isolated, separable subject, Levinas moves back from Heidegger to Husserl. As is well known, in *Being and Time,* Heidegger denies precisely Husserl's view of the ego, claiming that Husserl presents an ontic self, not an ontological one. In simpler terms, Husserl argues for a view of the ego as distinguishable from the historical self and the self's being-in-the-world. Heidegger, in contrast, maintains that the self only gains its identity *through its being-in-the-world.*

Significantly, Husserl makes his argument in *Cartesian Meditations* against Descartes's notion of the ego, which from Husserl's point of view remains too much a part of the world. As Husserl puts it against Descartes: "Just as the reduced Ego is not a piece of the world, so, conversely, neither the world nor any worldly Object is a piece of my Ego."[3] The notion that the ego is a piece of the world is, for Husserl, Descartes's great mistake, and while Descartes does at one point state that "sensation . . . is nothing but an act of consciousness,"[4] his claims about the ego's constitution remain too tied to sensibility for Husserl.[5] Husserl nonetheless believes that he has followed Descartes's method in describing what he calls the transcendental ego, which is defined by its *lack* of worldly attributes. Husserl thus affirms Descartes's *cogito* but gives it a new twist: "To say, 'I am, *ego cogito*', does not therefore mean I, this human being, am."[6] While Husserl argues that the transcendental ego isn't subject to personal pronouns, he also claims that

3. Husserl, *Cartesian Meditations,* 26. See also 69.
4. René Descartes, *Meditations on First Philosophy,* in *Descartes: Philosophical Writings,* trans. Elizabeth Anscombe and Peter Thomas Geach (Indianapolis: Bobbs-Merrill, 1971), 71.
5. See especially Husserl's Second Meditation.
6. *Cartesian Meditations,* 25, trans. mod.

the transcendental ego is at once absolute and unique.[7] A discussion of the ways in which Husserl tried to work this tension out is beyond the scope of this essay. What we need to appreciate, however, is that Husserl claims to be following Descartes in affirming a unique subject whose uniqueness derives from the stripping away (what Husserl called the "bracketing") of its historical and social situation. From Husserl's perspective, this further stripping away of the Cartesian *cogito* beyond any remnant of this world is consistent with, and in fact demanded by, the Cartesian method.

In *Being and Time*, Heidegger accepts Husserl's view of Descartes's legacy as epitomizing the modern, acontextual subject. When Heidegger criticizes the philosophical dichotomy between subject and object, he does so with Husserl and Descartes in mind. In order to show that from the perspective of being itself there are no absolutely separable subjects, Heidegger (perhaps somewhat ironically) restores to the ego the personal pronoun that Husserl had denied it. As Heidegger puts it: "Because *Dasein* has *in each case mineness* [*Jemeinigkeit*], one must always use a *personal* pronoun when one addresses it. 'I am', 'you are.' "[8] But the effect of Heidegger's restoring the personal pronoun to the ego is to show precisely that the ego cannot be described without reference to its social and historical relations. The ego, for Heidegger, is fundamentally relational. That I am I is only possible because I exist in a web of relations. Outside of these relations, there is no subject. So while Heidegger, in arguing against Husserl, might seem to be returning personal identity to the ego, he is, from another perspective, also denying precisely any notion of personal identity in the sense of absolute identity (which is what Husserl wants to affirm).

One might think that, based on his view of the primacy of ethics, Levinas's notion of the self would be closer to Heidegger's than to Husserl's. But Levinas maintains, *contra* Heidegger, that identity is not wholly relational but rather separable. In this, he returns to Husserl's notion of a truly separable self, though this self for Levinas is not an ego in terms of cognitive function. Rather, he argues that the truly unique, separate self is one that can be encountered phenomenologically only by way of an appreciation of sensibility and sensation. Unlike Husserl's transcendental ego, Levinas's ego is not a thinking self but a self that

7. See especially Fifth Meditation.
8. Martin Heidegger, *Being and Time*, trans. John Macquarrie and Edward Robinson (New York: Harper & Row, 1962), 68.

senses itself as uniquely separated from being. For Levinas, in order for the ego to think, it must first be separate from being, it must sense itself as itself.

It is the self's sense of itself *as a separable, independent self* that is the core philosophical argument of *Totality and Infinity.* Against Heidegger, Levinas maintains that there is a separable subject whose identity cannot be reduced to any web of relations. From Levinas's point of view, Heidegger's "mine" reduces the self to nothing, while Husserl's "mine" overly cognizes the identity of the ego. Levinas's attempt to make ethics first philosophy is captured in his "mine," which *contra* Husserl is not a cognitive matter and *contra* Heidegger transcends social and historical relations. Levinas's "mine" concerns my unique responsibility for the other person. This responsibility is "mine" alone and I am uniquely defined by it. I do not possess this responsibility; rather, this responsibility *is* me. But in being me, my unique responsibility requires a self who experiences itself as unique, *a self who stands outside of the social and historical order.* To begin to posit such a self, Levinas turns back from Heidegger to Husserl. But as we will see in the next section, it is ultimately from Husserl to Descartes that Levinas turns in order to describe a unique being that finds itself unique not in its cognitive existence but in its sentient existence. We will leave for the conclusion the question of how this sentient being is linked to Descartes's "I think therefore I am."

PART III: LEVINAS AND DESCARTES

Jean-Luc Marion has noted the concurrence between Heidegger's and Husserl's views of Descartes, despite their fundamental disagreement about the status of the ego. As Marion puts it:

> [T]his fundamental dispute with Husserl does not keep Heidegger from agreeing with him . . . : He consistently agrees to interpret Descartes' *cogito, ergo sum* in terms of . . . the representation that runs through intentionality. Only one difference remains. At the point where Husserl acknowledged an anticipation of phenomenology, Heidegger denounces a form of metaphysics. But whether they approve or disapprove of intentionality, they give the *cogito, ergo sum* the same interpretation in terms of it. . . . [T]hinking, *cogitare,* is equivalent . . . to putting thought at a distance as an object.[9]

9. Jean-Luc Marion, *Cartesian Questions,* trans. Daniel Garber (Chicago: University of Chicago Press, 1999), 99–100.

Marion shows that Descartes himself rejected the idea of intentionality that Husserl and Heidegger associate with his philosophy. Descartes, Marion argues, does not, *contra* Husserl and Heidegger, claim that every thought is accompanied by an "I think." As Descartes put it, this view of the cogito "is as deluded as our bricklayer's saying that a person who is skilled in architecture must employ a reflexive act to ponder on the fact that he has this skill before he can be an architect."[10] Marion follows Michel Henry in describing Descartes's *cogito* as "material phenomenology," by which he means to emphasize Descartes's focus not on intentionality and representation in grounding the "I," but on receptivity and sensation.

We cannot discuss here the complex philosophical and historical issues of Descartes scholarship in twentieth-century France. But this brief mention of Marion's discussion of Michel Henry's interpretation of Descartes provides us with an important starting point for understanding Levinas's view of Descartes. It is interesting that Marion does not refer to Levinas in this essay, first published in 1990, on Henry's reading of Descartes. While Levinas certainly does not give a comprehensive account or reading of Descartes or even of the *cogito,* the general theme of receptivity is the key to understanding Levinas's construction of the self. For Levinas, the self is not one who represents itself to itself through thought (the view that Husserl and Heidegger both attribute to Descartes). Rather, Levinas's self senses itself as itself by way of sensible experience. While not systematic in its presentation, the discussion of Descartes in *Totality and Infinity* provides the framework for Levinas's phenomenological description of the separate and independent subject.

As I argued in the beginning of this essay, Section II of *Totality and Infinity*, "Interiority and Economy," constitutes the core argument of the book, upon which the arguments in Sections III and IV are built. From the beginning, Levinas frames his effort in this section as an effort to find a middle point of sorts between Husserl and Heidegger. He criticizes Husserl's claim that every intentionality is founded upon representation, but states also that his goal is not to be "anti-intellectualist" like "the philosophers of existence," and Heidegger in particular, in understanding the existent only in terms of doing and labor.[11]

---

10. From Seventh Responses; quoted in Marion, 104.
11. For the characterization of Husserl, see the first paragraph of IIB, "Enjoyment and Representation." For the contrast with Heidegger, see the opening lines of IIA.

Levinas's description of the self is a return to Husserl's view of a trans-historical self, but by way of Heidegger. For all his analysis of the moods of *Dasein*, Heidegger, Levinas suggests, has not taken the mood of satisfaction seriously because he has reduced our understanding of things to their use. He argues, against Heideggerian phenomenology, that hunger is not related just to the need for food but also to the possibility of contentment.[12] In attempting a phenomenological analysis of contentment, which he also calls "enjoyment," Levinas stretches the limits of Husserl's notion of intentionality, claiming that the self senses itself as a separate, isolated, and independent self in a noncognitive way (*TI*, 134). Significantly, Levinas attributes the possibility of this analysis to Descartes: "The profundity of the Cartesian philosophy of the sensible consists, we have said, in affirming the irrational character of sensation, an idea forever without clarity or distinctness, belonging to the order of the useful and not of the true" (*TI*, 135). Levinas means to return to what he claims is the fullness of the Cartesian view of sensibility, which, he maintains, affords access to a reality that cognitive knowledge cannot reach. Sensibility, he contends, grounds the self "beyond instinct" and "beneath reason" (*TI*, 138). Sensibility does not constitute representation, which is the province of reason, but it does constitute what Levinas calls "the very contentment of existence" (*TI*, 135), which is my unreflective sense of myself. I do not possess sensibility but am constituted by it. Heidegger's *Da*, Levinas maintains, cannot account for sensibility: "It is not a care for Being, nor a relation with existents, nor even a negation of the world, but its accessibility in enjoyment" (*TI*, 138).

Before the self makes objects of the world, sensibility, for Levinas, is the receptive capacity of the self to bear and be shaped by the world in which it lives:

> The bit of earth that supports me is not only my object; it supports my experience of objects. . . . The relation with my site in this "stance" [*tenue*] precedes thought and labor. . . . My sensibility is here. In my position there is not the sentiment of localization, but the localization of my sensibility. . . . Sensibility is the very narrowness of life, the naïveté of the unreflective I, beyond instinct, beneath reason. [*TI*, 138]

---

12. "It is not that in the beginning there was hunger; the simultaneity of hunger and food constitutes the paradisiacal initial condition of enjoyment" (*TI*, 136).

Levinas claims that sensation is not the subjective counterpart to objectivity but is prior to objectivity. Sensibility is not muddled thought but gives access to a reality that reason cannot attain. A reality that serves no theoretical or practical purpose, contentment and enjoyment are the location of the trans-historical, trans-cognitive self. Levinas calls this sense of self a "surplus," for it cannot be captured by reason, biology, or society. Again using the example of eating, he writes:

> Eating, for example, is to be sure not reducible to the chemistry of alimentation. But eating also does not reduce itself to the set of gustative, olfactory, kinesthetic, and other sensations that would constitute the consciousness of eating. This sinking one's teeth into things, which the act of eating involves above all, measures . . . a surplus that is not quantitative, but is the way the I, the absolute commencement, is suspended on the non-I. [*TI*, 128–29]

Throughout Section II of *Totality and Infinity*, Levinas provides detailed analyses of the ways in which the "I" separates itself from the world in the surplus produced by sensibility. The "I," he insists, is a separate subject that cannot be subsumed into being or the objects of the world.

Again, Levinas claims to expand Husserl's notion of intentionality in order to describe a view of the self that cannot be reduced to its thought about itself or to the relations that constitute it. By turning to sensibility to describe how this self is constituted, Levinas also attempts to correct Husserl's correction of Descartes. While Husserl maintains that Descartes went wrong in understanding the ego as carrying with it a residue of the world, Levinas maintains that Descartes was right in grasping how the self as self is constituted by the world *before* it can begin to constitute the world. For Levinas, Husserl's desire for transcendental purity must be corrected by a return to this initial Cartesian insight. But this does not mitigate Levinas's notion that he is in keeping with Husserl's phenomenological method, which, unlike Heidegger's, is not, Levinas claims, anti-intellectualist. Like Husserl and Descartes before him, Levinas does not object to but affirms reason's ability, in Marion's words, to put thought "at a distance as an object." But unlike Husserl, and like Descartes, Levinas claims that there is more to the self than this representational capacity. We will return to this point below. For now, however, we need to focus on how Levinas's claims about the sensible self make possible his claims about ethics.

PART IV: THE SEPARABLE SELF AND ETHICS, OR DESCARTES ONCE AGAIN

Already in Section II, Levinas states the claim that will ground his argument about ethics in Section III, "Exteriority and the Face." He writes:

> The intentionality of enjoyment can be described by contrast with the intentionality of representation. It consists in holding on to the exteriority which the transcendental method involved in representation suspends. To hold on to exteriority is not simply equivalent to affirming the world, but is to posit oneself in it corporeally. . . . The body naked and indigent is the very reverting, irreducible to a thought, of representation to life, of the subjectivity that represents to life which is sustained by these representations and *lives of them;* its indigence—its needs—affirm "exteriority" as non-constituted, prior to all affirmation. [*TI*, 127]

Levinas's analysis of enjoyment has shown that the separable subject is made possible by the interiorization of sensible input. The separate self is therefore by definition for Levinas a receptive self. Yet we have seen that the self's interiorization of sensible experience does not mean that the self is nothing but sensible experience. Levinas's analysis of nourishment, discussed above, suggests that beyond the science of sensibility (what he calls biology), there is a remainder (a "surplus") that accounts for our very humanity. But for Levinas the surplus that constitutes the separable, independent "I" on the basis of sensible experience does not produce a substantive "I" but one whose very constitutedness and indebtedness to the exteriority that has made possible its interiority become ever more apparent.

It is in connection with this indebtedness to the external world that Levinas understands infinity and the ethical relation. Significantly, he attributes this movement from the interiority of the self to the exteriority of the face of the other not just to Descartes's notion of infinity but to the *cogito* itself:

> It is by reason of this operation of vertiginous descent unto the abyss . . . that the Cartesian *cogito* is not a reasoning in the ordinary sense of the term nor an intuition. Descartes enters into a work of infinite negation, which is indeed the work of the atheist subject that has broken with participation and that remains incapable of an affirmation (al-

though, by sensibility, disposed for agreeableness)—enters into a movement unto the abyss, vertiginously sweeping along the subject incapable of stopping itself. [*TI*, 93]

The "movement unto the abyss" is for Levinas an indicator of infinity and the ethical relation. The atheistic self, both as a metaphysical construct and as a philosophical argument, leads to infinity. The very make-up of the atheistic self (its metaphysical constitution) is rooted in infinity. If, as Levinas argues, the *cogito* is grounded upon the exteriority that it has made interior, then the *cogito* itself is made possible by way of an exteriority for which it cannot itself account. It is for this reason that Levinas maintains that "the Cartesian *cogito* is not a reasoning in the ordinary sense of the term nor an intuition." The Cartesian method marks a movement into the abyss of the exteriority that constitutes the ego. Against Husserl's and Heidegger's reading of the *cogito*, Levinas maintains that the true separateness of the subject, its interiorization of exteriority, gives way to the ethical relation.

As I have suggested, Levinas's argument about the separable self and infinity is also apparent in the structure of *Totality and Infinity:* if Section II is philosophically successful, if Levinas has described adequately the phenomenological expression of the separate self, then his arguments about exteriority and the face in Section III will follow. Philosophically, the structure of *Totality and Infinity* suggests a transcendental argument of sorts. If we take as true the description of the separable self, then we must recognize that this self is made possible only by way of its relationship to the face of another. Indeed, just as Kant argues in the transcendental deduction of the *Critique of Pure Reason* that the self's inner tracking of itself as self is made possible by an external world of objects (which we can't know anything about), so too Levinas maintains that the self's sense of its own interiority is made possible by the exteriority of infinity. While there surely are profound affinities between Levinas and Kant in their attempt to articulate a kind of ethical humanism,[13] it is significant that in making his transcendental argument in *Totality and Infinity*, Levinas, following Husserl, retains the Kantian transcendental methodology while turning back to Descartes. For Levinas, Descartes's notion of sensibility and its relation to infinity show the way to a true understanding of tran-

13. See Samuel Moyn's forthcoming *Origins of the Other: Emmanuel Levinas between Theology and Humanity, 1928–1961* for a detailed argument along these lines.

scendence, which Kant's transcendental idealism cannot fully apprehend. This isn't to say, however, that Levinas is claiming that Descartes's philosophy is identical to his own. Rather, just as his teacher Husserl does, Levinas maintains that Descartes and the Cartesian methodology anticipate philosophically certain insights that he hopes to explicate further. Again like Husserl, and Descartes before him, Levinas has as his project in *Totality and Infinity* the building of philosophical truth by way of a systematic methodology.

We can now appreciate, in the preface to *Totality and Infinity*, Levinas's description of the task of the book. *Totality and Infinity*, he writes, "presents itself as a defense of subjectivity, but it will apprehend subjectivity not at the level of its purely egoist protestation against totality, nor in its anguish before death, but as founded in the idea of infinity" (*TI*, 26). We have seen that Levinas's arguments about a subjectivity founded in the idea of infinity rest upon his reading of Descartes and his claim that Descartes's notion of the self can and must be rehabilitated for the purposes of contemporary philosophy. In contrast to the postmodern reading of Levinas, we see that Levinas's philosophical project is not to overcome assertions about the modern subject but to reassert the truth of such a construction. We cannot deny that Levinas's "self" is different from what has become the conventional reading of Descartes's *cogito*. Nonetheless, we cannot ignore the fact that Levinas attempts to develop his own philosophy on the coattails of Descartes.

V: A QUICK NOTE ON *OTHERWISE THAN BEING*

It may seem that Levinas subsequently gives up his aspiration to rehabilitate Descartes. One might argue that, even if *Totality and Infinity* makes an argument for the modern subject, in *Otherwise than Being* Levinas reverses himself in arguing for the other as the locus of identity. After all, his arguments, especially in what is perhaps the central chapter of that book, "Substitution," are attempts precisely to dislocate the modern self. Levinas's claim in *Otherwise than Being*, and especially in "Substitution," is that I do not constitute my own identity; the other does.

However, we should not be misled into concluding, from Levinas's claims in *Otherwise than Being* about the passivity of the self, that he means to overcome the notion of a separable, isolated subject. Were we to accept a reading that posits such a dichotomy between *Totality and*

Infinity and *Otherwise than Being*, we would be overlooking the fact that Levinas's central argument in *Otherwise than Being* is an argument about the meanings of sensibility. We have seen that his claims about an isolated, separable self are based on his arguments about sensibility as a kind of intentionality beyond instinct and beneath reason. In *Otherwise than Being*, Levinas makes this very same argument. In a footnote he writes:

> Inasmuch as an image is both the term and the incompletion of truth, sensibility, which is immediacy itself, becomes an image, one that is interpreted on the basis of knowledge. But our thesis is that sensibility has another signification in its immediacy. It is not limited to the function of being the image of the true. [*OB*, 188, n. 4]

"That sensibility has another signification" is the very argument that Levinas makes in *Totality and Infinity* about the separable subject. I argued above that if, in *Totality and Infinity*, Levinas succeeded in his argument that there is an isolated, trans-historical self, then his argument about ethics would follow. In *Otherwise than Being*, he makes the same argument about sensibility that he makes in *Totality and Infinity*. The difference is that in *Otherwise than Being* he begins with the ethical relation and not with the isolated subject. Nevertheless, he nowhere denies the truth of the isolated subject and in fact affirms it in his description of the ethical relation.

It is worth noting, in this context, the epigraph to Levinas's chapter on "Substitution." He quotes Paul Celan: "Ich bin du, wenn ich ich bin [I am you if I am I]" (*OB*, 99). In claiming that I am you (this is his argument about substitution), Levinas nonetheless maintains that I am I. Just as he argues in *Totality and Infinity* for the separable subject as well as for the authority of the other over the self, so he argues in *Otherwise than Being* for the other's authority over me as well as for my separable self. If Heidegger's motto in *Being and Time* is "Everyone is the other, and no one is himself,"[14] then Levinas's motto, following Celan, would be: "The other is the other and the self is itself. Only thereby can I be for the other."[15] Both of these claims about the truly separable nature of the other and the self are made possible by his contention that sensibility has a meaning before and beyond cognitive representation. I sense myself in sensibility but it is also by way of sensibility that the other comes to me. In neither case is this sensing

14. *Being and Time*, 165.
15. This formulation is my own.

cognitive in nature. Rather, Levinas claims, my sense of myself and my sense of the face of the other stem from the fact that I am a receptive and (in the language of *Otherwise than Being*) created creature. Even if Levinas's style and argument are less transcendental in *Otherwise than Being* than in *Totality and Infinity*, his description of ethics continues to be predicated on his claims about the significance of sensibility. It is Descartes whom Levinas credits and claims to return to in making these arguments.

CONCLUSION: WHY DOES THIS MATTER?

In his important essay on Levinas's use in *Totality and Infinity* of Descartes's evil genius, Robert Bernasconi comments that *Totality and Infinity* is a fractured text.[16] For Bernasconi, Levinas's reliance on Descartes serves to undo the hegemony of modern philosophy. By contrast, my suggestion in this essay is that Levinas's reliance on Descartes is at least as positive as negative, if not more so. While Levinas would certainly part ways with what has come to be the accepted reading of Descartes, he nonetheless defends what he takes to be Descartes's claim for the centrality of the subject. Far from presenting a postmodern retreat from the subject, Levinas affirms Descartes's modern subject for ethical purposes. Beyond the question of the status and meaning of Descartes for Levinas, this point helps us appreciate a central yet productive tension in Levinas's philosophy. For all of his claims for passivity, Levinas is in fact a defender of ethical agency. Like Descartes's, then, Levinas's philosophy stands or falls on his account of the separable, independent subject.

16. Bernasconi, "The Silent Anarchic World of the Evil Genius," 272.

SAMUEL MOYN

Transcendence, Morality, and History: Emmanuel Levinas and the Discovery of Søren Kierkegaard in France

> [I]n France he is all but unknown . . . [yet] Kierkegaard's ideas are fated to play a great role in the spiritual development of mankind. It is true that this role is of a special kind. He will hardly be accepted among the classics of philosophy . . . but his thought will find a place, unseen, in the hearts of men.
>
> —Lev Shestov[1]

> When she asked why I had chosen Kierkegaard as an object of study and I replied that I did not know, Rachel Bespaloff said: "But don't you realize? It is because you are a Jew."
>
> —Jean Wahl[2]

INTRODUCTION

To judge from his postwar essays on the subject, Emmanuel Levinas rejected the founder of existentialism with no little irritation. Where Søren Kierkegaard interpreted Isaac's binding, in *Fear and Trembling*, as a parable about the role of faith in taking the self beyond the merely ethical stage, Levinas suggested that it is not Abraham's hand, ready to bring the knife to his son's throat, but instead "Abraham's ear for hearing the voice" that best captures the intent of the biblical story. It "brought him back to the ethical order." As Levinas explained it: "That [Abraham] obeyed the first voice is astonishing: that he had sufficient

---

1. Lev Shestov, *Kierkegaard et la philosophie existentielle (Vox clamantis in deserto)* (Paris: Vrin, 1936), 35–36. Throughout this article, all translations are my own, unless indicated otherwise.
2. Jean Wahl, "Discours de clôture," in Éliane Amado-Valensi and Jean Halperin, eds., *La conscience juive. Données et débats: Textes des trois premiers Colloques d'intellectuels juifs de langue française organisés par la Section française du Congrès juif mondial* (Paris: Presses Universitaires de France, 1963), 225.

YFS 104, *Encounters with Levinas,* ed. Thomas Trezise, © 2004 by Yale University.

distance with respect to that obedience to hear the second voice—that is the essential."[3]

The conflict in biblical interpretation mirrors their difference in philosophical outlook. Where Kierkegaard recommended, in a famous phrase, the "teleological suspension of the ethical," Levinas has become celebrated for the recovery and reinstatement of morality in philosophy. Where Kierkegaard narrated the existential drama of the self, Levinas dedicated his attention, with equal but apparently opposite fervency, to the so-called other. "[H]e bequeathed to the history of philosophy," Levinas complained of the Danish thinker, "an exhibitionistic, immodest subjectivity" (PN, 76). Opposing the solitary—and in his view, narcissistic and melodramatic—quest of the knight of faith, Levinas recommended the calm and healthy solicitude of interpersonal morality, "[t]he responsibility that rids the I of its imperialism and egotism (even the egotism of salvation)" (PN, 73). The pious submission to the other: this adventure, for Levinas, is paradoxically the most adventurous one available to the self.

Yet when the matter is considered more closely and historically, Kierkegaard's philosophical contribution turns out in many respects to be a major if unexpected station on the long way to the human other. In his portrait of the infinite qualitative difference between God and man, Kierkegaard set a crucial precedent for the notion of human "alterity" that Levinas is so renowned for defending. And in severing the individual from the all-inclusiveness of the historical process so that the self could search for this strangely distant god, Kierkegaard anticipated Levinas's own opposition to a fully historical and world-immanent picture of human existence.

For his most passionate contemporary advocates, Levinas's doctrine of "the other" is an utterly novel and wholly convincing approach; it finally unseated a long-standing if not permanent Western bias for "the same." I doubt that either the historical presumption or the moral evaluation is entirely correct. In this essay, I will endeavor to show that it is possible to understand Levinas's philosophy as a secularizing improvisation on Kierkegaard's early call for the recovery of the other in divine form. But the Kierkegaardian precedent is responsible, I will sug-

---

3. These comments are from Emmanuel Levinas, "Existenz und Ethik," *Schweizer Monatshefte* 43 (May 1963): 170–77 and in Jean-Paul Sartre et al., *Kierkegaard vivant* (Paris: Gallimard, 1966), 232–34, 286–88, both rpt., the latter with important changes, in *Noms propres* (see PN, 74, 77).

gest, not only for some of the power but also for some of the poverty in
Levinas's philosophical ethics.

After a summary reconstruction of the French enthusiasm for
Kierkegaard's thought, I turn to two neglected episodes in Levinas's engagement with the interwar fashion. The essential purpose of the study
is to remember forgotten debates in order to assert their importance as
evidence regarding Levinas's development generally and the role that
Kierkegaard and Kierkegaardianism specifically played in it. The thesis throughout is that the Levinasian insistence on "transcendence"
has a conceptual history. The process through which it came to occupy
the center of Levinas's thought also, I hope, helps account for some
persisting mysteries about Levinas's conception of alterity. Just as
Kierkegaard's picture of the relationship between God and man is secularized by Levinas as the very image of intersubjectivity, making it an
essentially dyadic affair, Kierkegaard's absolute distinction between
self and history found itself transformed, in Levinas's hands, into just
as rigid a difference between morality and politics. If these mysteries
are understood as flaws, then the Kierkegaardian lessons that Levinas
learned may well turn out to have obstructed as much as they enabled
his insight.

THE FRENCH ENTHUSIASM FOR KIERKEGAARD

Levinas became a philosopher in the midst of Europe's interwar experience. Though Kierkegaard's work had percolated throughout the con-
tinent during the several decades after his death, it is really only thanks
to the German interwar discovery of his philosophy that he became the
canonical figure he remains today. It is possible, almost, to say that
Kierkegaard is a twentieth-century rather than a nineteenth-century
philosopher. "If we were to write a history of his fame," Hannah Arendt
observed in 1932,

> only the last fifteen years would concern us, but in those years his fame
> has spread with amazing speed. This fame rests on more than the dis-
> covery and belated appreciation of a great man who was wrongly ne-
> glected in his own time. We are not just making amends for not having
> done him justice earlier. Kierkegaard speaks with a contemporary
> voice; he speaks for an entire generation that is not reading him out of
> historical interest but for intensely personal reasons: *mea res agitur.*[4]

4. Hannah Arendt, "Søren Kierkegaard," *Frankfurter Zeitung,* 29 January 1932, rpt.

This enthusiasm for Kierkegaard's work, in turn, owed its success to the prominence of the major Kierkegaardian of post-World War I Europe: Karl Barth. The reception of Kierkegaard's thought, which came only in a drizzle up to the appropriation in Barth's *Epistle to the Romans* and related writings, is unthinkable without Barth's stormy personality and instant fame.[5] Then publications by and about the Dane poured forth from the German presses in a torrent. Kierkegaard has no doubt had no more significant heyday than in the German intellectual life of the 1920s. It is less well known, but the French had their own Kierkegaard enthusiasm—only, as with their reception of phenomenology, it occurred after a significant delay and with some creative garbling. But historically speaking, it may have proved more consequential as the font from which international "existentialism" eventually flowed. What I am arguing in this essay is that, paradoxically enough, it also contributed decisively to the more recent interest in philosophical ethics. A general overview is therefore in order.[6]

The translation of Kierkegaard into French had been spotty and often corrupt, especially by comparison to Germany where, by the mid-1920s, readers could benefit from the celebrated edition of Kierkegaard's complete works, translated by Hermann Gottsched and Christoph Schrempf, that the Jena publisher Eugen Diederichs brought out over the decade and a half ending in 1924. By contrast, only in 1932 did

---

in *Essays in Understanding, 1930–1954*, ed. Jerome Kohn, trans. Robert and Rita Kimber (New York: Harcourt, Brace & Co., 1993), 44.

5. The authoritative study of the Kierkegaard reception before Barth is Habib C. Malik, *Receiving Søren Kierkegaard: The Early Impact and Transmission of His Thought* (Washington, D.C.: Catholic University of America, 1997). On Barth's connection, see Anders Gemmers and August Messer, *Søren Kierkegaard und Karl Barth* (Stuttgart: Strecker und Schröder, 1925) and Egon Brinkschmidt, *Søren Kierkegaard und Karl Barth* (Neukirchen: Neukirchener Verlag, 1971).

6. I have drawn principally on the following accounts: Jean Mesnard, "Kierkegaard aux prises avec la conscience française," *Revue de littérature comparée* 9 (1955): 453–77; Nelly Viallaneix, "Lectures françaises," in Niels and Marie Thulstrup, eds., *Bibliotheca Kierkegaardiana*, vol. 8, *The Legacy and Interpretation of Kierkegaard* (Copenhagen: Reitzel, 1981), and Jean Wahl, "Kierkegaard: Son influence en France," *Revue danoise* (1951): 34–36. See also François Bousquet, "Kierkegaard dans la tradition théologique francophone," in Niels Jørgen Cappeløm and Jon Steward, eds., *Kierkegaard Revisited* (Berlin: Walter de Gruyter, 1997), and F. J. Belleskov Jansen, "The Study in France," in Marie Mikulová Thulstrup, ed., *Bibliotheca Kierkegaardiana*, vol. 15, *Kierkegaard Research* (Copenhagen: Reitzel, 1987). See also Jacques Maritain, "Aspects contemporains de la pensée religieuse (I)," *Fontaine* 31 (1943): 18–33, esp. 22–28 on Kierkegaard, Barth, and Shestov; in English as "Contemporary Renewals in the Modern World," in Maritain et al., *Religion and the Modern World* (Philadelphia: University of Pennsylvania Press, 1941).

a complete rendering of any one of Kierkegaard's many books first appear in France, *The Sickness unto Death* under the title *Traité du désespoir* in a translation by Jean Gâteau and Knud Ferlov. A complete edition appeared only decades later. There had been, it is true, scattered and fragmentary translations—as well as interpretive essays by Victor Basch and Henri Delacroix—before World War I.[7] Only around 1930, however, did anything change—and then, as Nelly Viallaneix observes, "everything changed."

The sociology of knowledge invalidates what Kierkegaard himself insinuates. While the reader's experience seems to be personal, a dialogue between himself and the text, it is usually intelligible only as part of a trend. "It is from this date forward," Viallaneix remarks of 1930, "that Kierkegaard's renown really spread in France—just at the same time as France entered a 'crisis' not only economic but social and political in form. The anxiety of these *années sombres*, nourished by the rise of Nazism and the expectation of a new war, made the Kierkegaardian myth powerful. Translations and interpretations multiplied." The kind of context that had made Kierkegaard (like Barth himself) so popular a decade earlier in a defeated Germany now came to a France wracked by depression and increasing political and social polarization. With due allowance for the salient differences between the two moments, it is nonetheless true that the political upheaval of these years helped foster, for many, the cultural mood so inseparable from the Kierkegaardian interest and enthusiasm on the German scene a decade earlier.[8]

In religious circles, the German enthusiasm had special impact on Protestant theology. In this case, the reception of Kierkegaard often blended almost indistinguishably with the apotheosis of Barth himself in French thought. The key Kierkegaardian texts in Barth's collection *The Word of God and the Word of Man* appeared in French in 1933.[9] The two major journals of French Protestantism—*Foi et vie* and *Le semeur*—likewise celebrated and debated Kierkegaard and Barth in the early 1930s. Denis de Rougemont, a Swiss writer with close links to

7. Henri Delacroix, "Søren Kierkegaard," *Revue de métaphysique et de morale* 8/4 (1900): 451–84; Victor Basch, "Un individualiste religieux, Søren Kierkegaard," *Grande revue* (1903): 281–320. Levinas knew these publications; see below.

8. Viallaneix, "Lectures françaises," 108–9. Similarly, Wahl himself says that "one can in fact see that [Kierkegaard's fame] has grown especially since about 1930" (Wahl, "Kierkegaard," 34).

9. Barth, *Parole de Dieu, parole humaine*, trans. Pierre Maury and Auguste Lavanchy (Paris: Editions "Je sers," 1933).

French Protestantism (as well as to the nascent Collège de Sociologie), not only published his own studies of Kierkegaard but also founded a theological review called *Hic et Nunc*, explicitly modeled on Kierkegaard's own controversial series of pamphlets, *The Moment*.[10]

Rougemont's collaborator in this editorial venture, later an important theorist of religion and Islam scholar named Henry Corbin, joined the fray, too, learning Danish and translating Barth as well as publishing a number of articles in *Hic et Nunc* in preparation for his important tract on the subject, which appeared in *Recherches philosophiques* in 1934. This article merits special mention in light of the theme of the nonhistorical individual. Corbin's article proved among the highest-profile introductions to the new German theology of the "wholly other" on the French scene. It made the Kierkegaardian case for transcendence and against history with vigor. "The twofold task of religious philosophy which emerged from the *Aufklärung*," Corbin explained, "was the insertion of divine transcendence into the flux of history and the reduction of human existence to a generality." But, Corbin insisted, "the testimony of dialectical theology tends to show definitively how divine transcendence, which is forever outside history, i.e. non-historical, can only *reveal* itself as a concrete relation to concrete men." For this reason, instead of allowing itself to be accessed through history, the transcendent other is in fact "the foundation of the historicity of every concrete individuality."[11] A frequent contributor to *Recherches philosophiques*, the famous (if short-lived) journal cofounded by his friend Alexandre Koyré, Levinas would, I believe, certainly have known of the article. But very little hangs on the connection: similar notions about the priority of the wholly other to history were soon to be everywhere.

Indeed, the Kierkegaard enthusiasm did not only penetrate theological circles; it also found a deep foothold in the philosophical discussions of the time. The Kierkegaardian influence on various German philosophers now discussed so intensely in France, leaving aside for a moment studies of Kierkegaard himself, could hardly have been more

10. See, for example, Denis de Rougemont, "Kierkegaard en France," *La nouvelle revue française* 46/273 (1936): 971–76. On *Hic et Nunc*, see Bernard Reymond, *Théologien ou prophète?: Les Francophones et Karl Barth avant 1945* (Lausanne: L'âge d'homme, 1985), chap. 7 and, for the manifesto of the journal, 231–33.

11. Corbin, "La théologie dialectique et l'histoire," *Recherches philosophiques* 3 (1933): 250–84, at 252. On Corbin's later significance, see Steven M. Wasserstrom, *Religion after Religion: Gersham Scholem, Mircea Eliade, and Henry Corbin at Eranos* (Princeton: Princeton University Press, 1999).

obvious—beginning with Heidegger himself. (Interestingly, none other than Henry Corbin translated the first—and for a long time, only—French collection of Heidegger's writings, a defective but important rendering.) The cumulative effects were immense. According to Paul Ricoeur, the years 1936–1940 were, thanks to the Kierkegaard enthusiasm, those of the starkest intellectual life in the last century—starkest, one might add, until the conversions from existentialism to structuralism and from structuralism to poststructuralism. Ricoeur goes so far as to comment that "Kierkegaard is at the origin of French existential phenomenology." Indeed, in a phenomenon that all the early "histories" of existentialism tacitly recognized, the Kierkegaard enthusiasm may provide one of the best general rubrics for making sense of the evolution of French thought as the 1930s waned. As neo-Kantianism fell, a kind of "neo-Kierkegaardianism" rushed into the void.[12]

Two figures, however, thanks to their book-length studies on the subject, were absolutely beyond question the most significant in the dissemination and popularization of Kierkegaard in intellectual circles. There was first of all the émigré Russian-Jewish thinker Lev Shestov (in Paris, "Léon Chestov"), who contributed not just individually but through his leadership of a coterie of loyal disciples. And, against the background established by all of the more minor figures, there towered the philosopher Jean Wahl (also of Jewish origin). His various "Kierkegaardian studies"—the phrase he used as the title of his 1938 collection of writings from the period—were not only most important in the Kierkegaard enthusiasm in France generally but, more directly for these purposes, they were critical for Levinas's philosophical development in particular.

As it happens, Levinas wrote about Shestov during the 1930s and counted Wahl among his closest friends (indeed, he eventually dedicated *Totality and Infinity* to Wahl and his wife Marcelle). Consequently, these two figures need to be given special attention. It was in writing about Shestov, as it turns out, that Levinas first had occasion to mention his own predecessor Franz Rosenzweig in print—in fact

12. Martin Heidegger, *Qu'est-ce que la métaphysique?: suivi d'extraits sur l'être et une conférence sur Hölderlin*, trans. Henry Corbin (Paris: Gallimard, 1938); Paul Ricoeur, "Philosopher après Kierkegaard," *Revue de théologie et de philosophie*, 3rd ser., 13 (1963): 292–316. Mesnard, however, sees Kierkegaard supplanted by Heidegger and Jaspers in the "cénacles" of Parisian existentialism. Mesnard, "Kierkegaard aux prises," 467. Mesnard published his own book on the Dane after the war: *Le vrai visage de Kierkegaard* (Paris: Beauchesne, 1948).

this comment dwelled on Rosenzweig in more detail than Levinas would accord him before (or even in!) *Totality and Infinity* itself. And it was in interacting with Wahl, I will suggest, that Levinas moved from the enthusiasm for Kierkegaard to thinking about transcendence in a way that steered this enthusiasm in a new direction. The figure whom everyone else saw as the distant progenitor of Martin Heidegger, Levinas wanted to conscript into his battle against this incontestably great but (briefly) National Socialist thinker. The Dane would correct the German.

LEVINAS'S INITIAL STATEMENT ON KIERKEGAARD

Lev Shestov (1866–1938, born Lev Isakovich Shvartzsman), once among the more prominent Jewish philosophers of the period, had been expelled from the new Soviet Union along with many other Russian intellectuals in 1922.[13] After sojourning for some time in Berlin, he settled definitively in Paris, where he taught at the university before he died in the late 1930s. (Paris counted as the most important center of the Russian diaspora; Vladimir Nabokov, for example, lived there when he wrote his first novel in English, *The Real Life of Sebastian Knight*.) Shestov became immensely fashionable in his old age.[14] All of his older works were translated; and while he continued to write in Russian, his new books typically first came into print in French (and sometimes German) editions, published by his friends and admirers, who made up a genuine pleiad of followers. Apparently, for example, Georges Bataille studied under Shestov; he assisted in the translation of one of his works. But the most significant and devoted of Shestov's followers were the Russian-born philosopher Rachel Bespaloff and the Romanian-born poet Benjamin Fondane (1898–1944, originally Benjamin Wechsler), both of whom came to live in Paris at the time; their published work in

13. It is noteworthy, for example, that an older English-language anthology of Jewish thinkers features the work of Shestov along with Rosenzweig and Buber. See Bernard Martin, ed., *Great Twentieth-Century Jewish Philosophers: Shestov, Rosenzweig, Buber* (New York: Macmillan, 1969). It is likewise interesting that one of the founders of another kind of enthusiasm once enthused about Shestov. See Irving Kristol, "All Things Are Possible: Selection from a Jewish Existentialist Thinker," *Commentary* (January 1952): 68–71.

14. See Benjamin Fondane, *Rencontres avec Léon Chestov* (Paris: Plasma, 1982) for a record of some of his many intellectual contacts. It appears from this book (138) that he had personal interactions with Levinas in some capacity. See also Michael Weingrad, "New Encounters with Leon Chestov," *Journal of Jewish Thought and Philosophy* (forthcoming) for connections to Bataille and to Walter Benjamin.

the 1930s featured both extensive appeals to Kierkegaard and elaborate homages to their more proximate intellectual master.[15]

Still, Shestov's direct influence outstripped that of all of his admirers. It is thanks to Shestov, for example, that Husserl initially came to be known in France, if only in the wildly distorted image available in the vituperative polemic Shestov aimed against the master of German phenomenology. Though it originally appeared in Russian in 1917, the attack only came to the attention of the West in 1926. The somewhat vulgar interpretation Shestov offered, to which Levinas's professor Jean Hering immediately responded, nonetheless had a certain impact in France, no doubt helping to sow Levinas's youthful interest in the subject, which climaxed in his dissertation on Husserl's philosophy a few years later.[16]

But Shestov's interests, especially by the time he settled in Paris, were wider. In the many books that appeared in the 1920s and 1930s, Shestov not only popularized proto-existentialist Russian writers like Chekhov, Dostoevsky, and Tolstoy, but also looked back to those who now appeared, from the perspective of the vanguard, to be the pioneering founders of this movement misunderstood in their own times: Blaise Pascal, Friedrich Nietzsche, and (of course) Kierkegaard himself.[17]

Shestov also argued for a new conception of Judaism that opposed

15. See esp. Fondane, *La conscience malheureuse* (Paris: Plasma, 1936), with articles on Shestov, Husserl, Kierkegaard, and Nietzsche; and Rachel Bespaloff, *Cheminements et carrefours* (Paris: Vrin, 1938), with articles on Kierkegaard and Nietzsche. Fondane died in Auschwitz in 1944. Bespaloff earned most fame through her other book *De l'Illiade*, pref. Jean Wahl (New York: Brentano's, 1943). In the English edition, *On the Iliad*, trans. Mary McCarthy (New York: Pantheon, 1945), Wahl's foreword is replaced by Hermann Broch's essay "The Style of the Mythical Age: An Introduction."

16. The feud began with Shestov, "Memento mori: A propos de la théorie de la connaissance d'Edmond Husserl," *Revue philosophique de la France et de l'étranger* (January–February 1926): 5–62, and left a long paper trail, which I omit. The best treatment is in Eugene H. Frickey, "The Origins of Phenomenology in France, 1920–1940" (Ph.D. diss., Indiana University, 1979), chap. 2; on the merits, see Ramona Fotiade, "Evidence et conscience: Léon Chestov et la critique existentielle de la théorie de l'évidence chez Husserl," in Nikita Struve, ed., *Léon Chestov: Un philosophe pas comme les autres?* (Paris: Institut d'études slaves, 1996). Levinas's thesis: *La théorie de l'intuition dans la phénoménologie de Husserl* (Paris: Vrin, 1930).

17. Shestov, *La nuit de Gesthemani: Essai sur la philosophie de Pascal*, trans. Boris de Schloezer (Paris: Grasset, 1923); *Les révélations de la mort: Dostoievsky—Tolstoy*, trans. Boris de Schloezer (Paris: Plon, 1923); *L'idée du bien chez Tolstoi et Nietzsche: Philosophie et prédication*, trans. T. Beresovski-Chestov and Georges Bataille (Paris: Editions du siècle, 1925); *La philosophie de la tragédie: Dostoiewsky et Nietzsche*, trans. Boris de Schloezer (Paris: J. Schiffrin, 1926).

it to, rather than synthesized it with, philosophy. This interpretation is epitomized in his *Athens and Jerusalem* of 1938, the two cities symbolizing for Shestov the absolute divide between the lies of reason and the truths of unreason. Shestov did not hesitate in the least to take up the charge of the latter against the dominance of the former. He saw the heritage of Greece in European culture as a misleading and tragic rationalism that, by refusing to admit the reality of the fundamental human experiences of terror, loneliness, uncertainty, and faith, left the individual all the more alone when they came.[18] It is therefore not surprising that Shestov could find a source of insight and inspiration in the antiphilosophical writings of Kierkegaard in particular.

Shestov's most important book for these purposes, *Kierkegaard et la philosophie existentielle (Vox clamantis in deserto)*, appeared in 1936, in a translation by Tatiana Rageot and Boris de Schloezer. The text, like the rest of Shestov's works of the period, provides a meditative approach, unclassifiable by the generic standards of today, that worked in the grip of passion and, undeterred by academic scruples, substituted the declamations of rhetoric for the proofs of reason. It emphasizes two points worth particular mention.

Most fundamentally, Shestov urged his strict distinction between and opposition of Western rationalism and "Eastern" faith. The blandishments of philosophy could never alter the truth that—as the subtitle of the book proposed—man is alone in a desert crying for no one to hear. The ultimate questions of existence revealed all philosophy as a pack of empty promises; only faith could hope to provide more viable answers—and precisely by refusing to comfort and reassure. This dismissal applied quite specifically to the domain of philosophy known as ethics: Western morality, especially if rooted in philosophical rationalism, the attempt to dictate formalized rules of action, only obstructed existential faith. The mistake of philosophy, Shestov insisted, is to lock out, in the service of inhuman abstraction, the absurdity of life at it is lived. The theoretical rules of morality could never apply to the actual situations of life as they are exigently experienced. "That is why," Shestov explained, "Kierkegaard turned, not to reason and morality, which demand resignation, but to the absurd and faith, which give their sanction to daring. His writings and sermons, raging, frenzied, violent, full of intensity, speak to us of nothing else: . . . a mad

18. Shestov, *Athènes et Jérusalem: un essai de philosophie religieuse,* trans. Boris de Schloezer (Paris: Flammarion, 1938).

flight from the god of the philosophers to the God of Abraham, the God of Isaac, the God of Jacob."[19] Accordingly, and as Kierkegaard had so brilliantly discovered, the entire program of ethics had to be rejected for the sake of a decisive faith in a "teleological suspension of the ethical."

Levinas's 1937 review of the book, which appeared soon after its publication, is an assessment not only of Shestov but also of the Kierkegaard enthusiasm quite generally. Though brief, Levinas's article shows how deeply he rejected many of Shestov's basic premises and with them an uncritical fashion. "Kierkegaard's fortunes are by no means a fad," Levinas acknowledged near the beginning:

> The moral crisis opened by the Great War has given men the sharp feeling of the *powerlessness* of reason and the critical disagreement between a rationalistic civilization and the exigencies of the particular soul lost in a generalized anonymity. It has put in question, despite the remarkable advancement of science and technology, the value, hitherto unopposed, of the Greek heritage. On this basis, in different forms, both irrationalism and doctrines of violence have been renewed.[20]

This passage, which one is entitled to interpret as a global evaluation of the relevance and risks of the Kierkegaard enthusiasm as a whole, is interesting because it appears to take a dim view of what everyone else seemed to find so exciting. Levinas did not hesitate to include Shestov in this verdict.

After summarizing the philosophical harvest of the Kierkegaard enthusiasm—which added up, he said, essentially to the thesis of the ineffability of the individual—Levinas wrote: "Whatever response one gives to all of these questions, they have to be posed. The internal signification of all of the events that constitute my existence has to be respected, before interpreting them as a function of the universal order as constructed by reason." It may not be too much to suggest that, for Levinas, while the questions they posed were legitimate, the answers given by Kierkegaard and Shestov were mistaken. At least, Levinas applied this verdict explicitly to the most important of their conclusions. While in the 1930s Levinas might have agreed with these figures that

---

19. Shestov, *Kierkegaard et la philosophie existentielle*, 383–84; cf. Ronald Grimsley, "Chestov," in *The Legacy and Interpretation of Kierkegaard*, 276–77.

20. The review is in (and all quotations are from) *Revue des études juives* 52/1–2 (July–December 1937): 139–41.

faith is the answer, he could not follow them, he continued, in their exclusive definition of faith as "an enterprise full of risks, a worried faith, a religion in which the certainties are always menaced and have to be justified again and again, in which, indeed, each instant, pristine and pathetic, stands for itself and there are only new beginnings."

It is true that Levinas shows a complimentary attitude toward Shestov in some parts of the review, praising him for the brilliance of his style and presentation and recommending the book to those who wanted to renew their Judaism "as a religion, if philological research on the past of the Jewish people cannot satisfy them and if sterile homages before the 'beauty of the Ten Commandments and the ethics of the prophets' have left them cold." The dominant sense of the review, however, is the polite rejection of Shestov and his view—"those who know Shestov's works and his battle for Jerusalem against Athens will not find it surprising," Levinas noted in passing—that knowledge counted only as an "abdication of and annoyance to faith." In the final analysis, one can say that Levinas's reaction to the Kierkegaard enthusiasm, at least insofar as he found it represented in Shestov's work, is somewhere between discriminating acceptance and outright rejection. Insofar as it blended with and added to the irrationalist currents of the time, Levinas found it immensely suspect.

But Levinas sounded another interesting note. Properly interpreted, Levinas said, Kierkegaard's thought looked "more subtle" than the enthusiasm that, retrieving it from the past, also distorted it to suit the present. One of the ways in which it appeared more complex to discriminating eyes than in the typical presentation in the course of the enthusiasm, Levinas explained, involved Kierkegaard's long love affair with that most central rationalist of the Western tradition: Socrates. This element of Kierkegaard's career—which began with a dissertation on Socratic irony—definitively separated him, Levinas argued, "from any vulgar irrationalism." While the Kierkegaard enthusiasm and existential philosophy more generally threatened to "break apart the synthesis of Greece and Judeo-Christianity which the Middle Ages assumed it had secured," Kierkegaard himself appeared to express a different conclusion. For better or worse, "European consciousness does not have the strength to forget Socrates." Whatever his reputation, Levinas never rejected philosophy. He would attempt to reform it, with Kierkegaard's help, turning the suspension of the ethical into the ground of ethics.

BEYOND FRANZ ROSENZWEIG:
THE THEME OF TRANSCENDENCE

Levinas's review of Shestov's Kierkegaardianism is equally important—perhaps more important—for another reason. It is Levinas's only
published mention of Franz Rosenzweig, not only in the 1930s, but also
in the two decades that followed. It is therefore important to record and
to interpret it properly. The review began:

> The thought of Søren Kierkegaard, the Danish philosopher who died in
> 1855, has experienced for several years now a rare fortune. Jaspers and
> Heidegger in Germany and Jean Wahl and Gabriel Marcel in France—
> these are a few of the names that allow one to measure the extent of an
> influence that also exercised itself, in a very obvious manner, on the
> only modern Jewish philosopher worthy of the name: Franz Rosen-
> zweig.

In calling Rosenzweig "the only modern Jewish philosopher worthy of
the name," Levinas tacitly suggested that Shestov does not deserve that
title. He made this implication explicit later in the review: "M.
Shestov, a Jewish philosopher, is not a philosopher of Judaism," Levinas wrote.

In light of the connection so often stressed in contemporary scholarship between Levinas and his great German-Jewish predecessor, one
might conclude that the Kierkegaard enthusiasm itself influenced Levinas only through Rosenzweig's appropriative transformation. In *The
Star of Redemption*, his enigmatic masterwork, Rosenzweig praised
Kierkegaard right at the start for "contest[ing] the Hegelian integration
of revelation into the whole."[21] But in Levinas's lukewarm evaluation
of the Kierkegaard enthusiasm, particularly the contribution it made
to the violent irrationalism of the time, Levinas clearly implies that if
he esteems Rosenzweig, it is either not for his allegiance to Kierkegaardianism or else for his transformation of the Danish philosopher's
legacy.

In what sense did Rosenzweig transform Kierkegaard? As the citation indicates, Rosenzweig followed Kierkegaard's hostility to "totality," the Hegelian notion that spirit serves as an all-encompassing forum for every aspect of human existence. But the Hegelian totality that

21. Franz Rosenzweig, *The Star of Redemption*, trans. William W. Hallo (New York:
Holt, Rinehart, Winston, 1971), 7; cf. Michael D. Oppenheim, "Søren Kierkegaard and
Franz Rosenzweig: The Movement from Philosophy to Religion" (Ph.D. diss., University
of California-Santa Barbara, 1976).

Kierkegaard shattered in one form, as Peter Eli Gordon has usefully emphasized, Rosenzweig reintegrated into a new one, speaking repeatedly, in his discussions of the Jewish community, of the "new unity" and the "new totality."[22] For Rosenzweig, as Levinas himself recognized, "the subjective protest is impotent" against the "historical necessity" that Hegel defended. Accordingly, Rosenzweig "remained Hegelian on one point," because he wanted a substitute for the merely subjective outcome of "Kierkegaard and the Kierkegaardians and their protest against imprisonment in the system or in history."[23] Levinas's jaundiced view of Kierkegaard, one might therefore conclude, simply followed Rosenzweig's own ultimate rejection of the Danish philosopher.

It is certainly true that Levinas adopted, out of allegiance to Rosenzweig, the Kierkegaardian opposition to Hegel while straining mightily to avoid the "subjectivist" result—what he derisively called "the vanity of a merely personal protest"—to which that opposition originally led in Kierkegaard's own works. And yet, one can find serious limits to the hypothesis of an exact continuation from Rosenzweig to Levinas. The contemporary penchant is to find the analogies between Rosenzweig and Levinas and to leave the matter there. But the more one looks, the more plausible other influences—including Kierkegaardian contributions—become in Levinas's formation.

There are important considerations on the level of context. As Levinas himself observed, there were no easy ways to avoid Kierkegaard even in the midst of Hegel's Parisian apotheosis in the period after the war.[24] The brief triumph of Kierkegaardian existentialism in the 1930s, a decade too often presented simplistically as the incubator for postwar Hegelianism (and communism), left an indelible impression even on movements dedicated to breaking with it unceremoniously. "Kierkegaard's philosophy has marked contemporary thought so deeply that the reservations and even the rejections it may elicit are yet forms of that influence," Levinas remarked in the 1960s.

> [T]he return of Hegelian thought and the fascination it holds are not solely attributable to the foundation it provides for the great political

22. See in general Peter Eli Gordon, *Rosenzweig and Heidegger: Between Judaism and German Philosophy* (Berkeley: University of California Press, forthcoming) for a portrait of Rosenzweig made in Heidegger's holist and communitarian image.

23. These remarks come from the colloquy that followed Levinas's presentation, "'Entre deux mondes' (Biographie spirituelle de Franz Rosenzweig)," in Lévy-Valensi and Halperin, eds., *La conscience juive*, 147.

24. Michael S. Roth, *Knowing and History: Appropriations of Hegel in Twentieth-Century France* (Ithaca: Cornell University Press, 1988).

questions of today. . . . Neo-Hegelianism derives a kind of nobility from its reaction against the exacerbated subjectivism of existence. After one hundred years of Kierkegaardian protest, one would like to get beyond that pathos. . . . I have the impression that the seductiveness of the later Heidegger for us, and also the attractiveness of neo-Hegelianism and Marxism, perhaps even of structuralism, comes—in part of course— from a reaction to that completely naked subjectivity that, in its desire to avoid losing itself in the universal, rejects all form. [*PN,* 71, 76]

The anti-existentialist animus that Levinas interestingly saw as providing some of the spiritual motivation for much recent French thought, from Marxism to structuralism, never fully exorcised the subjectivism of Kierkegaard's thought. But then there is good reason to suspect that Levinas is implicated in the phenomenon he himself identified: it is important to look for the ways in which the reservations Levinas expressed against (and indeed his eventual rejection of) Kierkegaard's thought were "yet forms of . . . influence."

This likelihood raised by the context is born out in an examination of the text. The best evidence for Levinas's preference for Kierkegaard over Rosenzweig in opposing Hegel is related to the word and concept of "transcendence." For better or worse, it is in fact quite difficult to find this notion in Rosenzweig's thought, for he explicitly and repeatedly ridiculed it. It is, he argued, "the old [thinking that] addressed the problem whether God is transcendent or immanent," whereas the new thinking that Rosenzweig advocated simply drops this inquiry.[25] By the starkest of contrasts, transcendence is a central term and concept in Levinas's thought. Just as important, Levinas offered the transcendent other in opposition to the communitarian picture of intersubjectivity to be found in Heideggerian theory and fascistic practice; yet it is just this alarming ideology of resolute communitarianism that Rosenzweig himself insistently advocated in the portrait of the Jewish community that concludes his masterpiece.[26]

25. Rosenzweig, "Das neue Denken," in *Kleinere Schriften* (Berlin: Schocken, 1937), 384.

26. Gordon argues that Rosenzweig is "alive to the 'we' of community as much as to the 'thou' of alterity," a commitment bringing him into proximity not just to Heidegger but also to Carl Schmitt. In *The Star of Redemption,* Gordon suggests, "Rosenzweig calls the founding decision of community 'dreadful' (*grauenhaft*), since the 'we' must expel the 'you' 'from its bright, melodious circle into the cold dread of the nothing.' . . . This notion of the 'We' points to Rosenzweig's profound disagreement with Levinas: For while Levinas contested totality on behalf of alterity, Rosenzweig found in Jewish solidarity a singular and self-sufficient 'Whole.' Rosenzweig was thus favorable to the very kind of holism Levinas rejected on principle" (unpublished manuscript).

Because he championed "transcendence"—the alterity of other people that resists any reduction to plenitudinous unity—Levinas's alternative to Hegel apparently took a direction very different from the communitarian holism that Rosenzweig himself adopted. Levinas hoped for an alternative to lonely subjectivity that did not remain true to Hegel *even on one point* by simply discovering, like Rosenzweig, a different kind of whole. If not from Rosenzweig, the point of view of transcendence then had to come from somewhere else.

In his many works, Levinas presented an image of intersubjectivity hardly secularized from the theological picture of man humiliated in the presence of the divine. If Levinas is still even partially following Rosenzweig in these matters (a point of controversy too difficult to enter into here), he is also, ironically, transforming him in a Kierkegaardian direction and preserving more of Kierkegaard's thought than Rosenzweig himself did. In his adoption of the point of view of "transcendence," Levinas did draw on the Christian Kierkegaard—if only through the decisive intermediation of an interwar Jew like himself.

JEAN WAHL AND THE DISCOVERY OF THE THEOLOGICAL OTHER

Born in 1888, Jean Wahl, a longtime Sorbonne professor, is one of the more neglected figures in twentieth-century French intellectual history. This omission deserves to be rectified, not least in Levinas studies: the acknowledgement of Rosenzweig's influence in *Totality and Infinity* is rarely left unemphasized when a similar homage to Wahl in the same book is invariably passed over in silence.

Wahl and Levinas likely met one another when they each spent the winter semester of 1928–29 in Freiburg studying at the feet of their phenomenological masters.[27] Levinas evoked his friend's personal demeanor and philosophical contribution most memorably at a posthumous conference in his honor. "That marvelous pointillism of Jean Wahl!" Levinas exclaimed. "What a strange effect it produces," he continued, likening it to "a child's question coming from the lips of the wisest of philosophers."

---

27. Wahl's notes on Heidegger's lectures later served as the basis for his authority in speaking about Heidegger in France and he cited them throughout his 1930s works. They also contributed to his own lecture courses in France on Heidegger, one of which has recently been published. See Wahl, *Introduction à la pensée de Heidegger: Cours donnés en Sorbonne de janvier à juin 1946* (Paris: Livre de poche, 1998).

In many cases, Jean Wahl may be defined as the child's question within the Trojan walls of thought. Or the shaft of light shining through the structures of doctrines, striking particular, sometimes unknown points, awakening the experience of the other philosopher in the untamed state, in which it has retained its freshness prior to becoming hardened into a system, before being buried in the depths of an intellectual construction, before the dulling of its sharp, burning punctuality.

Wahl's main contribution to French intellectual life, Levinas went on to contend, is not so much a finished system as "the rejection of the kind of thought that is content with exclusive systems."

It has been the forerunner of certain daring undertakings (which are not all unduly extreme) of current philosophy. It is fair to say that in France it has paved the way for a new kind of reader and writer in philosophy, and a new sort of book. With it, a blow was struck against the structure of the system, philosophy set up in the guise of a logical architecture, the philosopher's stronghold or domain: a hereditary domain, to be handed down to schools, disciples, epigones—an intellectual feudalism amplifying (or as some feel in our time, repressing) the meaningful and the reasonable.[28]

Wahl's revolt against system (and even meaning) may likewise make it difficult to specify his contribution to Levinas's own development; but the insight that the attack on the systematic pretensions is something Wahl inherited from Kierkegaard's complaints against Hegel may allow some further precision.

Wahl appears at practically every significant crossroads in the complicated midcentury transfer of German thought to France—that of the Kierkegaard enthusiasm not least. He had begun his philosophical career much earlier than Levinas with a thesis, directed by Henri Bergson and dedicated to him, on the subject of time in Descartes's work. He claimed to find in all of Descartes's important doctrines, from the treatment of the *cogito* to the science of movement, the novel presumption that perception took place in the space of an instant. In light of Bergson's new philosophy of time, Wahl seemed to suggest, assumptions about the nature of time that must have informed earlier philosophies

---

28. Levinas, "Jean Wahl: Sans avoir ni être," in Levinas et al., *Jean Wahl et Gabriel Marcel* (Paris: Beauchesne, 1976), 17–18, 27. The essay is rpt. in Levinas, *Hors sujet* (Saint Clément: Fata Morgana, 1987); the English citations here are from *Outside the Subject*, trans. Michael B. Smith (Stanford: Stanford University Press, 1994), 71 and 79.

had to be reinterpreted.[29] It is perhaps too much of a stretch to claim that this contribution on the notion of the "moment" in Descartes prepared him for his later Kierkegaardian researches. His next book, however, certainly did. He published *Le malheur de la conscience dans la philosophie de Hegel* in 1929; it provided a French perspective on the Hegelian *Jugendschriften* recently edited and published by Hermann Nohl, Johann Hoffmeister, and Georg Lasson that played such a signal role in the enthusiasm and reinterpretation of Hegel's philosophy in existential form (in tandem with the discovery and publication of Karl Marx's own "prescientific" and Hegelian *Economic and Philosophical Manuscripts*).[30] More importantly, Wahl's choice of topic and method were themselves indicative of his future trajectory. "Still more than with intellectual problems," Wahl argued in his preface,

> Hegel began with moral and religious problems. The examination of his youthful fragments undertaken in this book confirms the impression one has from reading the *Phenomenology*; in their light, that text will no longer seem like just the introduction to his doctrine but also as a culmination: the narration and conclusion of his years of formation and voyage through systems.

In other words, Wahl's choice of theme—the passages on the "unhappy consciousness" from the *Phenomenology of Spirit*, which he separated out in order to trace back through Hegel's youth—already, in a sense, identified his true interest in Kierkegaard or at least primed him for it. "Behind the philosopher," Wahl suggested, "one may discover the theologian; and behind the rationalist, the romantic."[31]

There is no reason, of course, to insist that all of Wahl's interests turn out actually to be about Kierkegaard; it is more the case that his work, whatever its subject, introduced figures in a heady existential brew that makes his ultimate attention to Kierkegaard seem almost foreordained. But he also presented Kierkegaard in a version almost inseparable not only from Hegel but also from Heidegger and Jaspers,

29. Wahl, *Du rôle de l'idée de l'instant dans la philosophie de Descartes* (Paris: Vrin, 1920).

30. Wahl, *Le malheur de la conscience dans la philosophie de Hegel* (Paris: Presses Universitaires de France, 1929).

31. Ibid., v, cf. 8, 194. As Wahl later argued openly, "Kierkegaard's thought is a protestation of unhappy consciousness against the very idea of the evolution in which Hegel considered that consciousness to have been surpassed" (*Études kierkegaardiennes* [Paris: Aubier, 1938] chap. 4, "La lutte contre le hégélianisme," 135). He later came around, writing that one "must be wary of attributing too much historical importance to the young Hegel" (*Petite histoire de l'"existentialisme"* [Paris: Club Maintenant, 1947], 23).

whom he likewise helped naturalize. As Jean Mesnard protested of Wahl's *Études kierkegaardiennes*, "[t]his book not only devotes a direct commentary of one hundred octavo pages to the study of Heidegger and Jaspers, it never stops recalling their presence—indeed, their superiority—in the course of all the many notes that ornament the bottoms of the pages."[32] The same allegation, if it is one, applies to Wahl's other famous work of the period, *Vers le concret*, which surveyed trends in philosophy around the world (including American pragmatism) but admitted, as of the third page, that Heidegger had in a sense drawn the consequences of all the new discoveries Wahl would detail—so much so that a comparison throughout would assist rather than obstruct the understanding.[33]

But how did he help prepare Levinas's project? Whatever his syncretism, it is Wahl's naturalization of Kierkegaard's insistence on the infinite qualitative difference between God and man, as well as his sense of the philosophical relevance of that theme for understanding the self, that will now seem like his most important contributions. The best example is provided by his article, reprinted in the *Études kierkegaardiennes*, on *The Concept of Anxiety*. In his summary, Wahl stressed how the experience of anxiety, and particularly the individual consciousness of sin, both invalidated all philosophies of immanence and made God's shattering transcendence an irrefutable fact of life. In their most quotidian behavior, people are confusedly searching for the other. Kierkegaard's question, as Wahl rightly explained, is therefore how to convert the role of this other in the economy of selfhood from a source of menace to the grounds of beatitude. The feeling of anxiety is "tied to *the other* that is at first the indeterminate atmosphere in which I move," but, if next "interiorized and particularized so that it coincides with what is *other* in myself," could become "the other who is highest, to the absolutely *other*."[34] In Wahl's rendition, it is the essence of existential therapy, already in Kierkegaard's work, to discover and to make a place for the other in the experience of the self. The route to solicitude for the other may run through narcissistic self-absorption; but the ultimate destination is by no means the self alone. As

32. Mesnard, "Kierkegaard aux prises avec la tradition française," 467–68.

33. Wahl, *Vers le concret: Études d'histoire de la philosophie contemporaine* (Paris: Vrin, 1932), 3n.1: "We will often refer to Heidegger, who was deeply aware of several of the ambitions of contemporary thought." The text (with footnote) had appeared as the lead item in the first number of *Recherches philosophiques* 1 (1931–32): 1–21.

34. Wahl, *Études kierkegaardiennes*, chap. 7, "Par l'angoisse vers la hauteur," 251.

Wahl put it during the war, "The Hegelian dialectic leads us towards a vision of the whole," while Kierkegaard's opposite approach results in "a sort of nude and blind contact with the Other."[35]

If Kierkegaard is a "solipsist" only so far as *human* others are concerned, then he would have to be not so much attacked as appropriated for simply human relations if a secular philosophy of intersubjectivity is the goal. But Wahl not only identified a kind of theological template for Levinas's doctrine in Kierkegaard's works; Wahl himself clearly meant to translate Kierkegaard to France in a philosophical and not simply theological register. Differently put, Wahl's interpretation went exactly in the opposite direction from the one that Shestov proposed: he hoped to make Kierkegaard a welcome guest at the philosophical table that Kierkegaard, on Shestov's reading, had intended to overturn.

Not surprisingly, as Wahl's book chapters appeared in article form throughout the 1930s, Shestov determined that this secular and philosophical appropriation had to be rejected root and branch. "Something needs to be said so that Wahl's 'interpretation' is not unopposed," Shestov complained in conversation with Benjamin Fondane.[36] When Shestov's articles did not interrupt Wahl's appropriation, Fondane, in a remarkably malicious review article that also attacked Bespaloff and de Rougemont, renewed the ferocious attack. He stormily attacked Wahl for the mistake of attempting to sever Kierkegaard's thought from theology, as when Wahl saw fit to praise Kierkegaard "even if the religious that he describes does not correspond to any reality." Yet Wahl's true error, apparently, lay elsewhere. Even more abominably, Wahl had reduced Kierkegaard to a theorist—of anxiety, sin, whatever—rather than understanding his books as *enactments* of faith. For Fondane as for Shestov, any reading and therefore writing about Kierkegaard required living with him through what he suffered and achieved. "I have learned that according to Wahl, Kierkegaard did thus and so. But what about you? For when I read you, my dear Wahl, I am interested more in you than in Kierkegaard himself; I want to know what *you* think, what *your* torments are, *your* disquietudes. . . . It is strange to say, but if you would speak about yourself, I would know better what you think of

---

35. Wahl, "Realism, Dialectic, and the Transcendent," *Philosophy and Phenomenological Research* 4/4 (June 1944): 498.

36. Fondane, *Rencontres avec Léon Chestov,* 83; cf. 127–28, 140–41, 143. By contrast, thirty years after their publication, Levinas acknowledged Wahl's *Études* in print as the product of "the most complete, penetrating, and philosophical of Kierkegaard's historians." Levinas, "Existenz und Ethik," 153n.1.

Kierkegaard."[37] In this debate among Jews about the meaning of Christian knighthood, the professorial Wahl did not oblige his critic. As indicated by his polite but firm response to this unprovoked attack, Wahl wanted to choose the way of rational philosophy rather than irrational faith; though he interested himself in Kierkegaard's existential analysis, he did not follow Kierkegaard in the same fideistic and committed sense that Shestov and his followers did.[38]

As their careers progressed, both Wahl and Levinas continued to show themselves actively interested in the possible detachment of transcendence from background theological conceptions. It is historically important that Wahl moved furthest in this direction and against Levinas's resistance—most clearly when he began, in the mid-1930s, to contribute to the vogue of the notion of transcendence by turning from historical commentator to independent philosopher.

THE QUEST FOR A SECULAR PHILOSOPHY OF TRANSCENDENCE

On 4 December 1937, Wahl staged an international event that Levinas later recalled as "his famous lecture [*sa fameuse communication*]."[39] Not surprisingly, this central debate in the French philosophical community of the 1930s concerned the secular fate of transcendence. Wahl's lecture, entitled "Subjectivity and Transcendence," appeared that year in the *Bulletin de la Société française de philosophie* along with the transcription of a colloquy among Wahl, Gabriel Marcel, and Nicholas Berdyaev, as well as written responses from Heidegger, Levinas, Bespaloff, de Rougemont, Karl Jaspers, Karl Löwith, and Raymond Aron, among others.[40] Levinas later paid homage to the book version of this debate—*Existence humaine et transcendance*, published only in 1944 in Switzerland—in his own most famous work, *Totality and Infinity* ("I have drawn much inspiration from the themes evoked in

---

37. Fondane, "Héraclite la pauvre; ou, Nécessité de Kierkegaard," *Cahiers du Sud* 22/177 (November 1935): 762, 765.
    38. Wahl, "A propos de Kierkegaard," *Cahiers du Sud* 22/178 (December 1935): 861–62. In a footnote, Wahl noted that he would accept neither the designation of "Kierkegaardian" nor that of "Kierkegaard's disciple."
    39. Levinas et al., *Jean Wahl*, 28.
    40. See *Bulletin de la Société française de philosophie* 37/5 (October–December 1937): 161–63, 166–211. By total coincidence, Léon Brunschvicg, the chairman of the session, announced the sad news that the same Henri Delacroix who had written the first analysis of Kierkegaard in France had died the previous day.

that study").[41] It provides unparalleled insight into the development of Levinas's ideas at this moment and in general.

The central question Wahl raised in his essays was whether Kierkegaard's theological conception of transcendence rules out a secular conception. He understood why some might doubt it in light of Kierkegaard's work. For while Kierkegaard "does not completely deny the 'other,' he often (not always) reduces existence to a meditation on a single other: God." The question had therefore to be posed. In attempting to bring the other into the world, Wahl asked, could the existentialist follower of Kierkegaard "completely deliver [himself] from the theological elements of Kierkegaardian thought?"[42]

Not everyone accepted the importance of this question. Denis de Rougemont offered this blunt rejection: "But why," he asked, "purify philosophy of theology? . . . For myself, I cannot conceive of any concrete relation with transcendence that lacked the touch of the divine or the sacred." Others showed deeper interest in the problems Wahl had posed. Berdyaev, in a move Levinas would also champion, insisted on the "very great difference" between the notion of transcendence and "the simple proposition that there is a reality beyond, an absolute reality, God, heaven, what have you. For transcendence is an existential experience or occurrence." The thrust of the debate in the 1930s is that, if theology is to be made philosophy, then transcendence defined as subjective experience will have to be detached from transcendence as mythologized in the various dogmatic propositions of the historical faiths.[43]

What is crucial for the intellectual historian in this debate, I want to argue, is the way in which Levinas resisted the penchant to understand Kierkegaard and Heidegger as continuous and instead cast the other's transcendence as portrayed by Kierkegaard as the fundamental alternative to Heidegger's immanent philosophy of being-in-the-world. Wahl's proposition had been that the contemporary existential-

41. See Wahl, *Existence humaine et transcendance* (Neuchâtel: Éditions de la Baconnière, 1944); Levinas, *TI*, 35n.2. Cf. Levinas, "Jean Wahl and Feeling," a review of Wahl's 1953 treatise on metaphysics (*PN*, 110–18).

42. *Bulletin de la Société française de philosophie*, 162. Kierkegaard, according to Wahl, left the problem not only whether this conception could admit of a secular translation but, even if it could, whether self and other would find themselves alone in their dyad to the exclusion of the world. Wahl also introduced a conceptual distinction between what he dubbed "transascendence" and "transdescendence" which, as the terms imply, have some directionality.

43. Ibid., 204, 187.

ists Heidegger and Jaspers appeared merely to "secularize" [*laïciser*] Kierkegaard's work; in wondering whether one could secularize Kierkegaard's "other," Wahl had missed the fact that for Heidegger the discovery of the other is not a goal, and transcendence is therefore fundamentally rethought. For Levinas, Wahl's formulation of the problem as one of secularizing translation understated the radicalism of Heidegger's attempt to abolish the problem of transcendence or, more accurately put, to substitute "ontological difference" for the intersubjective other (whether human or divine).

As background, it is crucial to know how Heidegger had dealt with the subject. In his important essay "On the Essence of the Ground," Heidegger had explicitly defined transcendence initially as *self*-transcendence, the refusal of the self to be like a static thing and as always in movement; and then, and more fundamentally, as transcendence from existents to existence.[44] These arguments marginalized not just the traditional religious definition of God's transcendence of the world, so important to Kierkegaard, but also *any possible secular theory of the transcendence of one existent over another.*

Levinas followed Berdyaev's appeal to the existential fact that some kinds of this interpersonal transcendence are rooted in experience, while the theologies of different religious sects are extrapolated from those more universal intimations. For Levinas, "the problems to which theology furnishes the solutions are entirely independent of it; they come into view by virtue of the simple fact that men exist." In other words, existential problems appeared to be those that both underwrote all sects and were therefore, in a sense, the subject they all presupposed and were really about before they diverged into controversy.[45]

More crucially, Levinas argued that the concept of transcendence is one that Heidegger had intended not to secularize but instead to overcome. For Levinas, "the form that existential philosophy takes in Heidegger's thought distances itself as far as possible from theology." He explained his definition of secularization: "Whatever the role of theology in Heidegger's intellectual formation, everyone should grant that, for him, to secularize a notion cannot simply mean camouflaging its religious dimension. *Secularization must involve an operation which ends by truly surpassing the theological point of view.*" The point at

---

44. Heidegger, "Vom Wesen des Grundes," *Jahrbuch für Philosophie und phänomenologische Forschung* 8 (1929): 1–138, rpt. in *Wegmarken* (Frankfurt: Klostermann, 1967).

45. *Bulletin de la Société*, 194.

which Heidegger made this attempt, Levinas said, counted as "the touchiest [*le plus névralgique*] of his philosophy."[46]

As Levinas argued, the discourse of the encountered other, whether in religious and theological or secular or existential form, is *ontic*. It concerned the "transcendence" between two beings. But the entire point, as well as the "great interest," of Heidegger's work, Levinas said, "consists in showing that at the base of man's *ontic* adventure there is something more than a relation of one 'existent' with another: there is the comprehension of being more fundamentally." And "human existence . . . only interests Heidegger because it allows a penetration to ontology." For Heidegger, human existence, and therefore the forum of religious or interpersonal transcendence, is (supposedly) not of independent interest.[47] At this point Levinas could draw his most important conclusion. For Heidegger, transcendence "does not mean . . . the relation [*passage*] of one 'existent' to another, but that of the existent towards being." Accordingly, "Heidegger breaks with theology exactly insofar as he makes the distinction between the ontic and the ontological (and he makes it with a radicalism without precedent in the history of philosophy)."[48]

While Levinas did not criticize Heidegger in so many words, there is more in the comments than simple clarification. There is a fundamental alternative presented in the way Levinas structured the prob-

46. Ibid. (emphasis added). In his letter, Löwith understood Heidegger's relation to theology to be even more paradoxical: "Jaspers's philosophy is, at bottom, *ersatz* religion, in spite of the fact that Jaspers is essentially an antitheological partisan of the Enlightenment. In contrast, Heidegger's philosophy is anti-Christian, in spite of the fact that— or even because—he has remained essentially a theologian. . . . In Heidegger, one still senses an immediately religious motivation at work—only it is perverted" (Ibid., 204). Löwith had contributed to the French Kierkegaard enthusiasm with his article, "L'achèvement de la philosophie classique par Hegel et sa dissolution chez Marx et Kierkegaard," *Recherches philosophiques* 4 (1934–35), later incorporated into his famous history of nineteenth-century thought, *From Hegel to Nietzsche*.

47. *Bulletin de la Société*, 194–95. Heidegger's intervention in the debate is not surprising in this light. Long before the *Letter on Humanism*, he wrote simply to say that, contrary to the conventional wisdom, he did not practice *Existenzphilosophie* and, in a prefiguration of his postwar *Letter*, to insist that "the question with which I am concerned is not that of man's existence; it is the question of being as a whole and by itself." As for the existentialism beginning to rule Paris, Heidegger said, it seemed exposed to the "twin danger that it will collapse into theology or else dissolve into abstraction." Wahl replied somewhat unconvincingly that, all the same, by Heidegger's own lights, existential philosophy provided the only means of approach to the problem of being. It seemed strange, to Wahl, for Heidegger now to disown what he had himself helped invent. Ibid., 193.

48. Ibid., 195.

lem. A choice has to be made. It determines what philosophical meaning, if any, "transcendence" will have. *Either* one remains at the level of the existent *or* one descends, with Heidegger, to the plane of being. *Either* the level of existents, and transcendence between and among them, *or* the plane of their being, and transcendence toward it. In effect, Levinas suggested that even the secular theory of interpersonal transcendence that Wahl wanted to develop presupposed the Kierkegaardian experience of the other's transcendence that, far from secularizing, Heidegger analytically marginalized.

Levinas did not join Wahl's quest for a secularized conception of transcendence as emphatically in the interwar debate as he would later; indeed, Levinas's 1937 comments suggest that a full commitment to secular philosophy might require the radical redefinition of transcendence that Heidegger offered. But a focus on this difference in the 1930s would occlude the deeper premise that Wahl and Levinas shared. It consisted in a preference for Kierkegaard's interpersonal definition of transcendence against the ontological definition that Heidegger pioneered. When Levinas later tried to make his own philosophy of intersubjective transcendence purely secular, he would do so, it bears noting, in spite of the implication of his own argument from the 1930s that an intersubjective definition of transcendence remained crypto-theological rather than secular, ultimately dependent on the relation between God and man that it tried to cast in purely human terms. Secularization must involve an operation that ends by truly surpassing the theological point of view.

KIERKEGAARD ALIVE

I have thus suggested that the philosophy of the other which is now so commonplace, in manifold forms, is historically speaking a kind of "ethical theology" (on the model of Carl Schmitt's political theology). Already in the interwar period, I have tried to show, Levinas came to defend a Kierkegaardian theology of self and other as an *alternative* to Heideggerian ontology (not its precursor). This essay must leave aside the interesting finale of Levinas's Kierkegaard journey except to note that he came to believe he had found a way to preserve the Kierkegaardian solicitude for the other without the theological foundation he had earlier supposed it might require.[49] Ironically, Levinas's mature de-

49. Samuel Moyn, *Origins of the Other: Emmanuel Levinas between Theology and Humanity, 1928–1961* (forthcoming).

fense of a purely human and secular ethics in *Totality and Infinity* brought him back to his own demand against Shestov for a rationalist Kierkegaard as well as to Wahl's project of finding a secular one.

Not that anyone paid attention to Levinas at the time. "In a sense," Georges Bataille perceptively noted, "Emmanuel Levinas has situated himself outside of 'French existentialism,' if that expression refers to a unified group epitomized by Sartre, Simone de Beauvoir, and Merleau-Ponty."[50] Levinas attempted a neo-Kierkegaardianism different enough from the reigning, Sartrean version of the fashion to be ignored for decades. In fact, the triumph of existentialism went so far that Levinas felt free to assimilate the Kierkegaard on whom he had drawn to the Heidegger and Sartre whom he philosophically rejected. When Jean Wahl—initially interned at Drancy[51] in 1941 and then, after a fortunate release, a professor at the New School and Mount Holyoke during the war—staged another colloquium in 1946 that, like the one the decade before, gathered many of the leaders of the Parisian philosophical field together for a contentious attempt to clarify together the spirit of the age, Levinas made evident his distance from the new movement, to the point of obscuring his recourse to one existentialist to respond to another.

In his interventions, Levinas reduced the Kierkegaard enthusiasm as it had occurred in Germany and France to Heidegger's thought, as if there were no point to discussing Kierkegaard and the controversy were really about Heidegger himself. It was as though, far from paving the way for Heidegger, as other interpreters argued, Kierkegaard had been revived only because he had approached, without reaching, the independent content of Heidegger's own analyses.

> It is possible that behind each phrase of Heidegger there is some Kierkegaardian thought—certainly, Kierkegaard was well known in Germany and even in France, as Henri Delacroix and Victor Basch had written on him at the beginning of this century—but it is thanks to Heidegger that this train of thought has sounded a philosophical note. I mean that, prior to Heidegger, Kierkegaard was confined to the provinces of essay, psychology, aesthetics, or theology, and that after Heidegger, he came into the purview of philosophy.

50. Georges Bataille, "De l'existentialisme au primat de l'économie," *Critique* 3/21 (February 1948): 126.
51. See Jean Wahl, "Poèmes (Drancy 1941)," *Fontaine* 32 (1944): 135–50, rpt. in Wahl, *Poèmes* (Montreal: Editions de l'Arbre, 1945).

In a sense, if Kierkegaard counted as important *philosophically*, it is only because Heidegger did first.[52]

And yet, Levinas's (questionable) historiographical assimilation of Kierkegaard to Heidegger in the postwar era may have led him to forget the interwar history of his own philosophical recourse to the Dane's search for the divine other in overcoming the German's all-too-human communitarianism. This recourse left clear legacies not just in his vocabulary—whenever he spoke of the "transcendence" of the "other"—but in his concepts, too. I have suggested how this occurred historically. And in Levinas's philosophical masterpiece, *Totality and Infinity*, the essence of Kierkegaard's defense of the individual against history and his depiction of the self's relation to a higher other remain strong—indeed, central—elements.

The rejection of history is prominent in the book among his opening moves. The viewpoint of morality, Levinas explained, is opposed to the Hegelian vision of politics, which necessarily involves the slaughter-bench. The irreducibility of the individual that Levinas calls, in *Totality and Infinity*, "separation," shows the limits of the Hegelian philosophy of history, which denies the significance of separation in order to integrate each individual into a larger story than himself. The consciousness of separation is different from—indeed, the disconfirmation of—the historical point of view. The self, thanks to separation, must always understand itself as *in medias res* and therefore unsublatable, even projectively, into some larger epic. The point of view of the last man, therefore, betrays the very history whose final meaning the Hegelian claims to deduce. The individual refuses to be reduced to "a pure loss figuring in an alien accounting system" of the recollective owl's sweeping comprehension of the whole. Instead, "[t]he real must not only be determined in its historical objectivity, but also from interior intentions, from the *secrecy* that interrupts the continuity of historical time" (*TI*, 56, 57–58).[53]

---

52. Wahl, *Petite histoire*, 83. As Wahl convincingly replied, this interpretation completely ignored important features of the enthusiasm: "It is not [necessarily] through Heidegger that one discovers Kierkegaard, even if, sociologically and historically speaking, many have done so (some people would not have cared to read Hegel if Marx had not existed). It is not from Heidegger that the historians of thought like Delacroix and Basch (and a good many Germans) found out about Kierkegaard. Moreover, many discovered him not through Heidegger but through Barth, whom Levinas has not mentioned." Ibid., 87.

53. Man "is uprooted from history," Levinas concluded, when he "truly approaches the other" (*TI*, 52). With apparent inconsistency, Levinas also remarked, a few pages ear-

As for the better known theme of the infinitely different and higher other, it is true that Levinas attempted, in his portrait of intersubjectivity, to "singularize" the ethical relation so that it would escape the strictures against generality that had led Kierkegaard himself to reject ethics. "Is the relation to the Other that entering into, and disappearing within, generality?" Levinas asked. *"That is what must be asked in opposition to Kierkegaard as well as in opposition to Hegel"* (PN, 72). But it is, in a sense, only by importing the singularity of what Kierkegaard found in the leap of faith to God back into the ethical stage that allowed Levinas to make this innovation. For Levinas, the unique alterity of the Kierkegaardian divine is to be found in every human other. Even as the French continued their obsession with Kierkegaard, as illustrated most dramatically by the Unesco conference of 1964 entitled "Kierkegaard Alive," Levinas had gone beyond Kierkegaard—but perhaps only, I have argued in this essay, thanks to partially Kierkgaardian means.[54]

EPILOGUE: BETWEEN MORALITY AND POLITICS

It thus turns out that the "immodest" Kierkegaard, transformed from a violent knight of faith to a peaceful emissary of morality, founded a crusade in theology that Levinas continued in ethics. If Kierkegaard's separation of the self and his hostility to history left profound legacies in Levinas's thought, these legacies were not always persuasive. They cast light, I believe, on the depth of Levinas's philosophical affiliation with the Kierkegaardian movement. Whether or not he valuably reconfigured Kierkegaard, Levinas's implausible distinction of individual morality from collective politics may have taken his affiliation with Kierkegaard too far.

The stark opposition of morality to politics appears most strikingly in Levinas's inaugural Talmudic readings of the early 1960s on the subject of Jewish messianism. In a creative interpretation of a debate between Shmuel and Jochanan in Tractate Sanhedrin, Levinas—not coincidentally—claimed to find an early version of the conflict between Hegelians and Kierkegaardians that obsessed his own contemporaries, the "proponents and adversaries of Marxism, that is, the entire think-

---

lier in the same book, that the encounter with the other takes place *"within* the totality and history" (TI, 23).

54. See the proceedings, Jean-Paul Sartre et al., *Kierkegaard vivant* (cited above).

ing world of this mid-twentieth century" (*PN*, 71).[55] In Levinas's view, Jochanan and Shmuel were debating whether the hypothetical end of history in the advent of the messianic age would lead to a complete resolution of human problems—moral as well as political—or whether, because human life is defined by the exigency of ethical commitment, moral problems can never disappear (*DF*, 62–63).

For the *marxisant* Jochanan, Levinas explains, the end of days is not just a political concept. It would, rather, bring the complete purification and regularization of human life. For Shmuel, in contrast, it is not expectable that moral problems will vanish in the messianic age.

> Contrary to Shmuel, who does not . . . separate the messianic era from the difficulties encountered by morality . . . Rabbi Jochanan envisages a pure and gracious spiritual life that is in some way stripped of the heavy load of things which is made concrete by economics. In his vision one can have direct relationships with the Other, who no longer appears as poor but as a friend; there are no more professions, only arts; and the economic repercussions of actions no longer have any bearing. Rabbi Jochanan in some way believes in the ideal of a disincarnated spirit, of total grace and harmony, an ideal exempt from any drama; while Shmuel, on the other hand, feels the permanent effort of renewal demanded by this spiritual life. [*DF*, 62–63]

Shmuel's beautiful position, with which Levinas clearly sympathizes, does not necessarily turn a blind eye to the difficulties of human inter-relationships, even though it denies that these are implicated in any way in the end of days. Instead, Shmuel reserves the perfection of human relationships on a moral level for "the future world" (it is not always familiar to Jews, Levinas remarks, that Judaism distinguishes between messianic times and the future world). Crucially, however, the future world is outside of history; for this reason, the end of history in the messianic days does not bring it about.

The domain of morality, then, is not and never history. The singularity of the interpersonal relation is distinguished and exempted from the vagaries of historical—and therefore political—life. As Levinas explains, for Shmuel the "future" world is paradoxically out of time. It "concerns a personal and intimate order, lying outside the achievements of history. . . . The future world cannot be announced by a

---

55. I have discussed what follows from a different angle and in more detail in "Emmanuel Levinas's Talmudic Readings: Between Tradition and Invention," *Prooftexts*, forthcoming.

prophet addressing everyone. . . . The personal salvation of men . . . escapes the indiscretion of the prophets; no one can fix in advance the itinerary of this adventure" (*DF*, 60–61). The exigencies of morality that everyone faces, in other words, are eternal rather than historical. The moral adventure—the real quest each person must discharge—is reserved for interpersonal intimacy rather than mass conflict. If obligations are to hold, it is not going to be up to politics and history and collectives; it is going to be up to each person alone. The personal is, precisely, not political.

In such passages, Levinas is evidently following Rosenzweig: improvising, like his predecessor, on the exilic topos of Israel the witness to the nations, the haven of perpetuity subsisting peacefully in the midst of the internecine belligerence of the powers, eternal witnesses to their merely historical conflicts. But whereas Rosenzweig is a particularist, Levinas is a universalist. Insofar as Levinas wanted to extend the monitory and testimonial role that Rosenzweig reserved to Jews to the individual subject of any faith or none, one can find Kierkegaard too—the suprasectarian and post-Christian Kierkegaard with whom several important philosophers of Jewish origin identified (or whom they partly invented) in the interwar period. It is not beside the point that Jews played such a surprising and prominent role in the French Kierkegaard enthusiasm of the age. "Hitler," the Kierkegaardian Albert Camus later went so far as to exclaim, "was history in its purest form."[56] The Kierkegaard enthusiasm helped Levinas to the point of arguing, beyond and against Rosenzweig, that there is a Jew in each person and he is morality.

The all-consuming cataclysm of the war, and the turbulence that has ensued, have in many quarters made Levinas's non- or suprahistorical ethics attractive. It may even have an unexpected but real compatibility with the widespread contemporary fatigue with ideology, which is a reminder that the same periods that allow concerned moralists to come to the fore are often just as propitious for self-congratulatory moralizers. In this regard, it is interesting to note that even in the immediate postwar and post-Holocaust age, many—including many Jews—insisted on the stubborn tendency of history to resume and rejected the standpoint of pure morality as altogether too comfortable to believe or to accept. The restoration of Levinas's Talmudic readings

56. Albert Camus, *The Rebel: An Essay on Man in Revolt*, tr. Anthony Bower (New York: Vintage, 1954), 150.

from his book *Difficult Freedom* to the colloquies in which they began shows that the battle of Hegel and Kierkegaard continued to rage and that not everyone took Levinas's side. Politics, some insisted, is not the opposite of morality but rather the true forum of moral opportunity. Wladimir Rabi complained, in response to Levinas's presentation, that "it is simply an alibi to search for eternity, for it amounts to the refusal of choice before the problems that interest the modern world." And even if Levinas's interest in restricting the scope of politics turns out to have been shared by many of his coreligionists, the lengths to which he took his Kierkegaardian perspective did not win universal assent. It seemed to his audience that the very importance of morality justified a different and more compatible understanding of politics than Levinas articulated. Émile Touati, for example, asked whether it is, in the end, possible to distinguish the two realms; Robert Aron wondered whether the exclusion of the Jews from history ignored the role messianism accords to human beings to participate in God's design through politics and hasten the end of days; the veteran Wahl, always present, objected similarly, and in spite of his Kierkegaardian credentials, to the "pretense" involved in the wish to live outside of history.[57]

These criticisms point to potentially severe defects in the approach that makes the availability of the other in ethics depend on the immunity of the moral from the historical and the ethical from the political. In the Marxist atmosphere of Parisian intellectual life in the crucial decade of the 1950s, when Levinas's thought climaxed, the Kierkegaardian opposition to history and politics may have functioned as a useful antidote to an immoral fashion. But that the Hegelian obsession may not have justified the Kierkegaardian vogue even then is suggested by the book-length indictment of the movement in the début of the American liberal Judith Shklar. "In his beautiful defense of the eternally human values of indignation against revolutions justified by historical reason," Shklar commented in *After Utopia*, her panoramic reconstruction of the thought of a host of significant figures in the period, "Kierkegaard's disgust at Hegel's bland systematization of evil [returns]." As she insightfully argued, this disgust often seemed purely

---

57. Lévy-Valensi and Halperin, eds., *La conscience juive*, 138, 287–88, 144. Levinas's promising response: "An 'existence outside of history' . . . does not mean, as M. W. Rabi supposes, the comfort of neutrality, of passive expectation, of non-engagement, the ivory tower, the perspective of Sirius. . . . To live an eternal life is to have the power of judging history without waiting for it to end" (Ibid., 147). Cf. Lévy-Valensi and Halperin, eds., *La conscience juive face à l'histoire* (Paris: Presses Universitaires de France, 1965), 3–148.

reactive, leading into the blind alley of "alienation," a result as potentially nefarious as the *engagement* it simply reversed. "Totalitarian-
ism," she commented, "has only intensified the romantic's sense of
apartness from history. . . . [I]n this extreme alienation lies also an admission of futility, for history is now too far from [him] to be even understood."[58]

Is this remark applicable to Levinas's *Betrachtungen eines Unpoli-
tischen*, rooted as they are in the same Kierkegaardian movements, produced during the same period, and in response to the same threats?[59]
In response to the danger that it is, I will conclude by noting the obvious. The polarization between morality and politics creates the mistaken impression that while morality is safe and certain, beautiful and
perfect, politics is shadowy and fallen, even soiled and dirty. Yet even
eternal moral principles, should they turn out to exist, would require
a politics; indeed, one could say that the belief in their immediate relevance to the political world is itself a moral necessity. One may un-
derstandably want to ask, in response to the much-discussed "ethical
turn" among Western intellectuals, whether a moral doctrine that
claims to be outside and above politics is plausible on moral grounds.[60]

But more fundamentally and troublingly, I think, it is implausible
to distinguish entirely or shield completely the domain of interpersonal and face-to-face transactions where Levinas saw morality oper-

58. Judith N. Shklar, *After Utopia: The Decline of Political Faith* (Princeton: Princeton University Press, 1957), 130.

59. Cf. Fritz R. Stern, "The Political Consequences of the Unpolitical German," in
The Failure of Illiberalism: Essays on the Political Culture of Modern Germany (New
York: Knopf, 1971). It is interesting that Levinas attempted to preserve the *grounds* for
Rosenzweig's opposition to Zionism in his own Zionist vision. One possible criticism of
this version of Zionism is obvious: by adopting the fiction that Jews are not political, it
is blind to their inevitably political actions.

60. There are many forms of the excessively acute contrast between morality and politics. As Michael Ignatieff has noted, "[h]uman rights activism likes to portray itself as
an anti-politics, in defense of universal moral claims meant to delegitimize 'political'
(i.e., ideological or sectarian) justifications for the abuse of human beings," but this self-
understanding is an "illusion." Ignatieff et al., *Human Rights as Politics and Idolatry,*
ed. Amy Gutmann (Princeton: Princeton University Press, 2001), 9, 29. Meanwhile
Jacques Derrida's preservation of the strict opposition between morality and politics (or
justice and law) in his attempt to outline a politics of the Levinasian other seems to lead
only (in Dominick LaCapra's apt description) "in the direction of an unguardedly hyper-
bolic stress on the enigmatic call of an open or empty utopia" and to "the hope-against
hope of . . . a messianic, ecstatic, even wonder-struck expectancy whose fulfillment is
impossible or endlessly deferred." LaCapra, *Writing History, Writing Trauma* (Baltimore:
Johns Hopkins University Press, 2001), 197, 218. Both comments suggest the need for a
more immediate connection or blurred distinction between morality and politics.

ating from mass politics and collective history. If a transhistorical theory of intersubjectivity, such as the one Levinas offered, is important to develop, it has to be a theory open to (if not compatible with) the lesson of modern social theory that the profoundest intimacies of human interactions are affected by their historical moment and tinged and often tainted by the power relationships of collective politics. In coming to a skeptical point of view on the premise that morality and politics are absolutely and generically different, one may well want to avoid the equal and opposite extreme, Friedrich Engels's irresponsible emphatic rejection of "any moral dogma whatsoever as an eternal, ultimate, and forever immutable ethical law on the pretext that the moral world . . . has its permanent principles which stand above history."[61] All the same, *la morale pour la morale* seems little better than *la politique pour la politique.* A beautiful soul is no real substitute for dirty hands.

It is perhaps a great irony, but it is nonetheless true, that Kierkegaard has, through Levinas's appropriation, inadvertently but in the end incontestably helped teach European philosophy how to be moral. Yet just as each person must learn to live, somehow, both in biographical and historical time, each must learn, somehow, to be more than moral. The viewpoint of morality, though it is essential, is by itself not enough. The line between morality and politics, because it is relative, is constantly and necessarily crossed. If so, this activity, even when undertaken in the name of the morality Levinas movingly defended, will have to occur in spite of his immunization of the self from history and the truths of ethics from the affairs of the day. There is a burden of responsibility, but there is even more to shoulder.

61. As cited from the *Anti-Dühring* in Steven Lukes, *Marxism and Morality* (Oxford: Clarendon Press, 1985), 11. Lukes argues that Hegel's and Marx's (and Jochanan's?) subordination of morality to politics, though from one point of view an attack on morality, is from another perspective simply a different moral vision.

ALAIN TOUMAYAN

"I more than the others":
Dostoevsky and Levinas

Throughout his work and in many interviews discussing it, Levinas has recourse to a broad panoply of aesthetic references as well as to an array of common, straightforward metaphors to translate his ideas. Among the literary references that Levinas has most frequently and consistently employed to try to express his unusual conception of ethics is a reference to Dostoevsky's *The Brothers Karamazov*, a quotation that Levinas's biographer, Marie-Anne Lescourret, goes so far as to characterize as his mantra or talismanic quotation, "sa citation fétiche."[1] In Chapter V of *Otherwise than Being*, Levinas, describing the situation of subjectivity as an accusative that is prior to any nominative, and playing on the multiple meanings of the verb "accuser," illustrates this configuration of subjectivity in the following manner: " 'Each of us is guilty before everyone for everyone, and I more than the others,' writes Dostoevsky in *The Brothers Karamazov*" (*OB*, 146). In other writings and in numerous interviews, Levinas alludes to this particular quote, modifying it occasionally and elaborating certain of its features in order to illustrate saliently various dimensions of his concepts of subjectivity and ethics, most often the notion of asymmetry or nonreciprocity that it expresses so radically and so strikingly (and that Levinas employs to distinguish his thought from Martin Buber's I/Thou),[2] but also the manner in which this asymmetrical "more than

1. Marie-Anne Lescourret, *Emmanuel Levinas* (Paris: Flammarion, 1994), 46–47. See Lescourret 43, 125, 356, as well as *The Levinas Reader*, ed. Seán Hand (Oxford: Blackwell, 1989), 1; Jill Robbins, *Altered Reading* (Chicago: University of Chicago Press, 1999), 147; and Robert Bernasconi, "What is the question to which 'substitution' is the answer?" in *The Cambridge Companion to Levinas*, ed. Simon Critchley and Robert Bernasconi (Cambridge: Cambridge University Press, 2002), 239.
2. "Interview with François Poirié (1986)," in *Is It Righteous to Be?: Interviews with Emmanuel Levinas*, ed. Jill Robbins (Stanford: Stanford University Press, 2001), 72–73;

YFS 104, *Encounters with Levinas*, ed. Thomas Trezise, © 2004 by Yale University.

all the others," in the second meaning of the verb "accuser" (to show or reveal), *singularizes, identifies,* or *elects* the speaking subject (*OG*, 72–73; *GDT,* 187; *TO,* 108). In interviews in *Entre nous* and *Ethics and Infinity,* and in an extended interview with François Poirié, Levinas alternates the notions of guilt, answerability, and responsibility within this formula while preserving its basic expression of asymmetry and nonreciprocity. Hence, in a variation that is, indeed, authorized by Dostoevsky's text (Dostoevsky uses most frequently *vinovatyi,* which means both guilty and responsible), he says that we are all "guilty" or we are all "responsible," always underscoring the coda, "I more than all the others."[3]

In this essay, I will examine Levinas's particular quotation of Dostoevsky in the general context of Book VI of *The Brothers Karamazov.* My purpose will be first to examine the appropriateness of this quote, given its context, to Levinas's repeated use of it in the formulation or translation of his ethical definitions in *Otherwise than Being* and elsewhere. Second, I will examine the extent to which other elements of Zosima's soliloquy, in particular the elaboration of ethical principles by means of figures of fraternity, servitude, and the face, relate to Levinas's use of the same figures in his formulations of the ethical. Such a correspondence would suggest the broad influence of Dostoevsky's novel in articulating salient ethical problems in French thought in the twentieth century. Indeed, referring to the character of Ivan, Sartre has deemed *The Brothers Karamazov* the "starting point" of existentialism,[4] while Camus, also focusing on Ivan, has remarked that with it "the history of contemporary nihilism really begins."[5] To the extent that the novel also supplies Levinas with elements of the answers that he will provide to both existentialism and nihilism, Dostoevsky's

---

Emmanuel Levinas and Richard Kearney, "Dialogue with Emmanuel Levinas," in *Face to Face with Levinas,* ed. Richard A. Cohen (Albany: State University of New York Press, 1986), 31.

3. Note that the variation between *"responsable"* and *"coupable"* in Levinas's allusions to Dostoevsky is not expressed in Robbins's translation, which carries "guilty" in both instances (François Poirié, *Emmanuel Levinas: Qui êtes-vous?* [Lyon: La Manufacture, 1987], 103, 123–24, and Robbins, *Is It Righteous to Be?,* 56, 72). On the translation of Dostoevsky's statement as "I have sinned," see Victor Terras, *A Karamazov Companion: Commentary on the Genesis, Language, and Style of Dostoevsky's Novel* (Madison: University of Wisconsin Press, 1981), 248 n. 21, 252 n. 70, 259 n. 156.

4. Jean-Paul Sartre, *Existentialism and Human Emotions,* trans. Bernard Frechtman (Secaucus: Citadel Press, 1998), 22.

5. Albert Camus, *The Rebel: An Essay on Man in Revolt,* trans. Anthony Bower (New York: Vintage, 1991), 57.

novel can be said to frame a debate which has had a defining influence on French thought in the second half of the twentieth century.

Mikhail Bakhtin's thesis concerning the essential polyphony of Dostoevsky's novels or the dialogism of the modern novel in general remains an insight that is fundamental to consideration of this novel (Terras, 85–87).[6] And the citation that Levinas occasionally attributes to Alexei Karamazov (OG, 84; Cohen, 31) is, itself, a salient example of the layered dialogism of Dostoevsky's composition. While the phrase is, in fact, "recorded" by Alexei, it is not his. The phrase belongs to Zosima. However, as uttered by Zosima, it is a quotation which, as he is dying, he recalls from his brother Markel, who expressed this idea as he himself was dying of consumption as a youth of seventeen when Zosima was eight (Robbins, Altered Reading, 147). The phrase is explicitly deemed unreasonable and extravagant, marshaled, in fact, as evidence that the illness to which Markel would presently succumb had, in the words of his physician, " 'affected his brain.' "[7] Zosima's narrative, through its force and authority, will, however, both explicitly acknowledge and concretely demonstrate the prophetic character of Markel's words. Indeed, Markel's pronouncement (it must be recalled that these are the words of a young man of seventeen) will be appropriated, endorsed, and repeated by Zosima who, as he is dying at the age of sixty-five, is not only indisputably in full possession of his faculties but is explicitly vouchsafing his legacy, and transmitting his blessing and his charge, to his disciples, Alexei among them. Indeed, initially characterized as outlandish, these ideas will become the primary solution to the formidable ethical challenges posed by the character Ivan to which, it will be recalled, not only Zosima's specific soliloquy but the entire novel, according to Dostoevsky, is conceived as a response (Terras, 6, 48).[8]

Now, the notions of unlimited answerability and responsibility will be the principal answer given in theory (through Zosima), in practice (through Alexei), and by example (principally Dmitry) to Ivan's doctrine of unlimited "lawfulness." In other words, to Ivan's doctrine of

6. See also W. J. Leatherbarrow, Fyodor Dostoevsky: "The Brothers Karamazov" (Cambridge: Cambridge University Press, 1992), 88–97, and Michael Holquist, Dostoevsky and the Novel (Princeton: Princeton University Press, 1977), 174.

7. Fyodor Dostoevsky, The Brothers Karamazov, trans. Andrew R. MacAndrew (New York: Bantam, 1970), 348.

8. See also Joseph Frank, Dostoevsky: The Mantle of the Prophet, 1871–1881 (Princeton: Princeton University Press, 2002), 570–71, 622.

freedom (so important for such thinkers as Sartre), and to his metaphysical revolt before the suffering of innocents (so important to Camus), will be placed, in counterpoint, Markel's, Zosima's, and Alexei's principle of responsibility and answerability (Robbins, *Altered Reading,* 148).[9] This, in simplified form, outlines the fundamental moral conflict of *The Brothers Karamazov* (Terras, 103), and it is a conflict that, as I shall suggest, is relevant to Levinas both in its broadest outlines and in very specific images that express it. The assertion of responsibility for the other, placed in Zosima's speech and thus in counterpoint to Ivan's theories presented in the chapters "Rebellion" and "The Grand Inquisitor," will find further expression and confirmation in subsequent episodes of the novel: for example, in the context of Zosima's narrative; in the story of his mysterious visitor, Mikhail; and, more significantly in terms of the novel's basic plot structure, in Dmitry's moral renewal or "regeneration," which enacts the novel's epigraph and which is contingent upon his acceptance of guilt for a crime he did not commit and responsibility for the suffering of innocents beyond his control, as his observations concerning a dream about a suffering child demonstrate:

> Thus I might restore an angel to life and bring back a hero! There are many of them, and we all bear the responsibility for them! Otherwise, why should I have dreamt about that "babe" at such a moment? And so I will go to Siberia because of that "babe," since every one of us is responsible for everyone else. We bear the guilt for all the "babes" because we are all children, small or grown-up, we are all "babes." I'll go and suffer for all of them, because someone, after all, has to pay for all the others. I didn't kill father, but I accept the guilt and I must suffer. [711]

This theme pertains even to the character Ivan. His rescuing of a drunk peasant in the snow, following his third interview with Smerdyakov, signals a growing and developing ethical consciousness, though one he is unable to acknowledge since it is at odds with his ideas, a conflict that will be expressed in his subsequent interview with the devil.

As noted, the principle of unlimited answerability or responsibility is presented explicitly in both counterpoint and in response to Ivan's doctrine of atheistic freedom.[10] The particular freedom that Ivan de-

---

9. See Richard J. Bernstein, "Evil and the Temptation of Theodicy," in Critchley and Bernasconi, *The Cambridge Companion to Levinas,* 257–58.

10. This principle actually precedes Ivan's discussions in the chapters "Rebellion" and "The Grand Inquisitor." In an earlier soliloquy, also recorded by Alexei, Zosima de-

scribes, and that seems to follow logically from or to be the moral expression of Ivan's doctrine that in the absence of God "all is lawful," is a freedom of independence, autonomy, particularity, and (incidently in Zosima's general characterization of it, which is very consonant with Levinas) an isolation that can only be transcended through the principle of answerability (366, 379, 380–81, 387).

Thus, Ivan's comments on the conflict between his half-brother Dmitry and his father (e.g., " 'If one wild beast devours another, it's good riddance to both of them' " [168; see also 171, 224, 825]) are in direct opposition to the attitude of responsibility for the other advocated by Zosima. The ethical emptiness of Ivan's argument expresses itself in a series of statements that reproduce Cain's answer to God in Genesis 4:9. This answer is given by Smerdyakov (271) and immediately afterwards by Ivan (278)[11] when Alexei is seeking Dmitry, by Perkhotin, to whom an exalted Dmitry has made rather obvious his intention of committing suicide and who nevertheless lets Dmitry leave for Mokroye with his pistols, with the repeated justification: " 'I'm not his nurse' " (493), as well as by Rakitin, who undermines his own moral high ground during his testimony at Dmitry's trial with the self-serving argument: " 'I cannot be held answerable for every person I know' " (804), and whose symbolic association with Judas is evoked in the episode to which he refers (434). It even, to some extent, though in a much more limited manner, indicts Alexei, who remained engrossed in conversation with Ivan when he should have been seeking out Dmitry (Terras, 74).

Levinas typically provides two exemplary cases of the antithesis of the ethical attitude: they are, on the one hand, from *Hamlet* ("What's Hecuba to him, or he to Hecuba / That he should weep for her?" [2.2 561–62]) and on the other, Cain's answer to God. In fact, the reference to Cain's answer to God could plausibly be characterized as the other side of the coin of Levinas's favorite quotation from *The Brothers Karamazov*, given the frequency and consistency with which he evokes it. And while this reference occurs almost as frequently as the quote concerning responsibility, only once, to my knowledge, does Levinas ex-

---

velops this idea of unlimited answerability, though without the striking formula "I more than all the others" (196).

11. The proximity of the two statements by Smerdyakov and Ivan consolidates the association of both characters in Frank's view (602). On the other hand, the fact that Ivan, as opposed to Smerdyakov, indicates an awareness that he is repeating Cain's phrase (" 'Does that sound to you like Cain's answer to God about his murdered brother?' " [278]) can also serve to distinguish him from Smerdyakov in a very significant way.

plicitly associate it with Dostoevsky. In a footnote in *God, Death, and Time*, citing and associating, as he frequently does, Cain's answer and Hamlet's, Levinas observes: "This is the response that Cain gives to God in Genesis 4:9. Dostoyevski places it in Ivan's mouth in *The Brothers Karamazov*" (*GDT*, 278, n. 11).

That the story of Cain and Abel and Dostoevsky's novel enact dramas of fraternity explains the leitmotiv of this reply in *The Brothers Karamazov*. And since fraternity will be one of the important figures that Levinas uses to express his ethical notion of responsibility for the other, the prevalence of this reference in his work will not be surprising, especially given his inclination to find examples in, and to cite from, the Old Testament. On the other hand, the extent to which Levinas's examinations of Cain's attitude describe with precision and accuracy the ethical limitations embodied by Ivan (and the other characters mentioned above, with the exception of Alexei) is very notable: "Human biological fraternity—considered with sober, Cainesque coldness—is not a sufficient reason for me to be responsible for a separate being; sober, Cainesque coldness consists in thinking responsibility on the basis of freedom or according to a contract" (*OG*, 71). Indeed, in describing his notion of responsibility in *Otherwise than Being*, Levinas distinguishes it from "the limited—and egotistical— horizon [*destin*] of the one who exists only *for himself* and washes his hands of the faults and misfortunes that do not begin in his own freedom or in his present [le destin limité—et égoïste—de celui qui n'est que *pour soi* et se lave les mains des fautes et malheurs qui ne commencent pas dans sa liberté ou dans son présent]" (*OB*, 116). In this, he describes Ivan's attitude and the moral horizon of his position. Again, in an interview, "Philosophy, Justice, and Love," in *Entre nous*, Levinas expands this analysis, now incorporating a polemic directed at Heidegger (which illustrates the association, in Levinas's mind, of ontology and freedom and the fundamental incompatibility of both with the ethical): "Cain's answer is sincere. Ethics is the only thing lacking in his answer; there is only ontology: I am I and he is he. We are ontologically separate beings" (*EN*, 110). Finally, Levinas's notion of responsibility, and one of his most provocative images of it, that of the hostage (which, as the image suggests, involves a responsibility that supersedes and subordinates the notion of freedom to the point of annihilating it), is articulated in the rhetorical terms of Cain's answer, as its negation: "The proximity of the neighbor is my responsibility for him: to approach is to be the guardian of one's brother, to be the guardian of one's brother is to be his hostage. This is immediacy. Responsibility does not come from fraternity, it is fraternity that gives responsibility for the other its name, prior to my freedom" (*OG,* 72).

Levinas's extensive reliance on Dostoevsky to characterize both positively[12] and negatively his principles of ethics suggests that the influence of *The Brothers Karamazov* and the influence of its principal ethical debate extend beyond the single quotation from Book VI of the novel. An investigation of the ethical dimensions of thè relation of servitude—certainly one of the principal axes of social, moral, and political thought since the Enlightenment—is another point on which Levinas's thought presents a striking parallelism with Dostoevsky's. Among Levinas's attempts to formulate the asymmetry or nonreciprocal character of the ethical relation is a superiority of the other that is examined in various figures, including the relation of servitude. For example, in the essay "The I and Totality" (1954), which, as its title indicates, lays some of the foundations of *Totality and Infinity* (1961), Levinas entertains and explores various intersubjective formulations of this relation. Although he will later significantly revise (if he retains it at all) the intersubjective terminology of the following analysis (deemed by him, in retrospect, to be "excessively ontological"), the Biblical overtones that are present will be retained, developed and, indeed, generalized. In the following, somewhat complicated analysis, Levinas examines the notion of respect through the relation of an intersubjective "commandment": "To respect cannot mean to subject oneself [*s'assujettir*], and yet the other commands me. I am commanded, that is, recognized as capable of a work. To respect is not to bow down before the law, but before a being who commands a work from me. But for this commandment to entail no humiliation—which would deprive me of the very possibility of respecting—the commandment I receive must also be the commandment to command the one who commands me. It consists in commanding a being to command me" (*EN,* 35). This particular model is given a fuller development in *Totality and Infinity* (*TI,* 212–13), in a context that makes much more explicit, on the one hand, Levinas's reference to Hegel (he uses the word "*maître*" several times), and on the other, his desire to formulate this problem in terms

---

12. Levinas acknowledges this reliance quite explicitly: "I always quote Dostoevsky" (Robbins, *Is It Righteous to Be?,* 100); "I always recall Dostoevsky in this connection" (*EN,* 105); "It is Dostoevsky's formula which I cite once more, as you see" (*EN* 107); "I return to my quote of Dostoevsky" (Pierre-Jean Labarrière, *Autrement que savoir: Emmanuel Levinas* [Paris: Editions Osiris, 1988], 72).

irreducible to Hegelian ones ("The relation with the Other . . . is not exposed to the allergy that afflicts the Same in a totality and upon which the Hegelian dialectic rests" [*TI*, 203]).

The conspicuous convolution of such formulations (apparent linguistically in their unusual repetitiveness, which we observe also in *Totality and Infinity:* "commandement qui commande de commander") suggests that they represent an attempt to solve a specific problem, which I would characterize as follows: Can a model of intersubjective subordination thus involving, de facto, hierarchy within a relation of power, be cast in such as way as to disable or cancel this relation, and thereby to resist thematization within the dialectical terms of Hegel's analysis of domination and servitude? Levinas's solution, made more striking through the use of a performative example with obvious Biblical overtones, is perhaps inelegant, but appears to work. In these scenarios in which, on the one hand, any authority I may exercise over another necessarily entails my commanding the other to exercise authority over my authority (in other words, the exercise of authority necessarily involves yielding it) and, on the other, any commandment I receive and to which I submit necessarily incorporates the command to command the one commanding me, the principle of power is mobilized specifically in order to cancel itself, and the principle of dialectic is undermined. This leads us back to Zosima and, specifically, to the inspired, prophetic words of Markel in *The Brothers Karamazov*. Here is how Zosima recalls Markel's words:

> To the servants who entered his room, he kept saying, "Why must you wait on me like this, my dear friends? Do you really think I deserve to be waited on by you? If God spares me for now and I go on living, I'll wait on you too, for we should all wait on each other."
>
> Mother listened to him, shaking her head. "It's your illness that makes you talk like this, my dear."
>
> "My dearest, beloved mother," he said, "since it is impossible to do without masters and servants in the world, let me also be a servant to my servants, just as they are to me. And I'll tell you also, mother dear— we are all guilty toward others and I am the guiltiest of all." [347]

Before the surprised reaction of his mother, Markel rephrases his words: " 'Know that this is the truth and that every one of us is answerable for everyone else and for everything' " (347). These are, as previously noted, the eccentric and extreme observations that make the doctor conclude that Markel " 'is not long for this world—his illness has affected his brain now' " (348).

As Zosima's narrative returns to the story of his life, he recalls his own youth in a manner that is very evocative of Dmitry's and recounts a "fateful" event that would "change the course of [his] life" (356). On the eve of a duel he had provoked for an imagined slight to his vanity, Zosima beats his orderly, a man named Afanasy, who does not resist or respond to his mistreatment at Zosima's hands. Zosima's remorse for this event triggers an epiphany that Markel's words frame and explain:

> Suddenly the words of my brother Markel came back to me, the words he had spoken before his death, when he had asked the servants why they were so kind to him and waited on him, and had wondered if he deserved their services. And I asked myself: "Do I deserve to be waited on? Why should another man, made in the image of the Lord, just like me, be my servant?" It was the first time this question had arisen in my mind. And I remembered my brother Markel saying, " . . . every one of us is answerable for everyone else. . . . " I felt tears come to my eyes and I thought: "Perhaps I am really guilty before everyone; indeed, I must be guiltier and worse than anybody else in the world." [358–59]

Having then bravely subjected himself to the first shot of his adversary in the duel, Zosima apologizes to him for his behavior and, amid the general commotion provoked by this breach of protocol, announces his vocation as a monk and his intention to enter the monastery. In the last chapter of his soliloquy, in which he summarizes his thoughts and teachings, Zosima returns to this question with a further anecdote about Afanasy. Eight years after the incident he described, he happened upon his former orderly, now married with two small children and living modestly but decently in a small provincial town. The reunion is sentimental and touching, involving the exchange of a "loving, brotherly embrace" and a "true communion of souls," and as they part, his former orderly gives him money destined both for his monastery and for Zosima personally, alms which Zosima accepts. This anecdote prompts a general reflection on the condition of servitude in which, again, Zosima acknowledges Markel's influence: "But the words I had heard from my brother as a child came back to me," and Zosima now expresses, in his own name, Markel's ideas to his assembled disciples: "Since the world cannot exist without servants, you must see to it that your servant feels freer in spirit than if he were not a servant. And why shouldn't I be my servant's servant?" (383–84).

To assert that this formula of becoming one's servant's servant offers a basic structural analogy with Levinas's "commandment that commands commanding" is not to suggest that Levinas might be here quoting Dostoevsky (although one will note that the formula occurs in the context of the citation about guilt and answerability), but to observe that Levinas and Dostoevsky have proposed structurally similar manners of resolving the problem referred to above: How, while acknowledging a relation of intersubjective hierarchy (" 'since it is impossible to do without masters and servants in the world' "), does one bring this relation to disable itself? Levinas, of course, examines the problem in a much more abstract manner than Dostoevsky, who has an immediate, concrete, and politically risky view of the question—even Zosima backs off somewhat from this proposition (Frank, 630)—and is no doubt less interested than Levinas in sidestepping any Hegelian formulation of the problem. However, the striking parallelism in the implied problem, the proposed solution, and the means of formulating the solution derive no doubt from a significant congruence in the ethical positions of Zosima with those that Levinas is elaborating.

As noted above, Levinas will not retain the model of servitude as a figure of the intersubjective relation. But this model will be retained as the basis of subjectivity, albeit at a higher level of abstraction. Thus, the images of subjection ("*s'assujettir*") and submission, rejected in the example above as an intersubjective principle, will become in *Otherwise than Being* the primary formula of subjectivity in a sense that is now transcendentally determined. In other words, the intersubjective horizon of the relation of subordination is raised to the higher power of transcendence. Thus, the commanding in the previous example becomes "ordination," which, Levinas reminds us, in French means to receive orders and to be consecrated (*EN*, 111). Receiving a divine command, responding to God's order, the figures of diaconate [*la diaconie*], submission (*OB*, 118), and subjection (*OB*, 117, 127) all become the very principles, bases, and conditions of subjectivity. Isaiah, who, for Levinas, saliently illustrates the principle of an accusative that precedes and supercedes any nominative, embodies this idea (*OB*, 199, n. 11).

Perhaps the figure that most consistently, forcefully, and creatively expresses the problem of intersubjectivity in Levinas is the face. This is a very extensive axis of Levinas's ethical investigations and it cannot be summarized here. But one of the fascinating and very original characteristics of the face in Levinas's thought is the manner in which it explicitly articulates a nexus of intersubjectivity and the transcendental. Indeed, among the principal characteristics of the face are its absolute alterity and incommensurability, whereby the face is not just analogous to, but a very expression of, the otherness of the divine. In the essay "The Trace of the Other," Levinas examines such features of the face, qualifying its mode of appearance in such terms as "epiphany" and "visitation" (which expresses the divine character of the event more forcefully in French than it does in English). He writes, for example: "A face is of itself a visitation and transcendence" (*DC*, 359). In this essay and elsewhere, he itemizes and describes the absolute foreignness of the face's provenance through spatial, temporal, and conceptual images: "A face *enters* our world from an absolutely alien sphere" (*DC*, 352); its temporal horizon is an immemorial past or even the eternal ("It is an immemorial past—and this also is perhaps eternity" [*DC*, 355]); and it is our immediate and concrete experience of the infinite (*TI*, 197, 199).

Interestingly, Russian, which, it will be recalled, is Levinas's native language, distinguishes between *lik*, the face in an abstract and implicitly transcendental sense, and *litsó*, the face in a more concrete, immediate, and conceptual sense of natural recognition or legal identification. Dictionary definitions of *lik* imply this transcendence in such examples as the representation of a face on an icon or the face of the moon, whereas the word *litsó* corresponds to more common, concrete meanings of the word "face" (Terras, 246, n. 1). The word *lik* is conspicuously used in two instances in the following passage of Zosima's soliloquy, in which Zosima, through an explicit description of Alexei's face in the mode of a visitation, and emphasizing its transcendental, mysterious, and prophetic character, introduces his brother, Markel, into his narrative:

"Fathers and teachers," the elder then said, turning to his visitors with a warm smile, "never until this day, not even to him, have I revealed why the face [*lik*] of this youth is so dear to my heart. But I will tell you now. His face [*lik*] is like a reminder and a prophecy to me. At the dawn of my life, when I was still a very small boy, I had an older brother who died in his youth, before my eyes, when he was only seventeen. And later, in the course of my life, I realized that this brother was like a sign to me, like a message from above, for if he had not come into my life, if he had not existed, I do not believe I would ever have taken monastic orders and followed a path that is so precious to me. And now the face that first appeared to me in my childhood has made a second appearance as I near the end of my life, as if it were a reminder. It is strange, fathers and teachers—although Alexei's face bears only a limited resemblance to my brother's, I have felt the resemblance in spirit to be so great that to me he has often been that other boy, my brother, coming to me mysteriously as I reach the end of my journey, to remind me of the past and to inspire me. I have even been surprised at this strange, dreamy feeling in me." [343]

In response to François Poirié's question: "What led you to philosophy?" Levinas answers that it was the Russian novel, especially the novels of Dostoevsky, in which characters are motivated by acute existential and religious anxiety—an anxiety over essential questions, fundamental problems, the meaning of life (Robbins, *Is It Righteous to Be?*, 28; see also Lescourret, 53–54, and Robbins, *Altered Reading*, xix). The preceding examples are intended to suggest that the connection of Levinas's formulations of ethical questions to Dostoevsky's novel surpasses the single, repeated allusion that provides Levinas with a rich and striking image of the asymmetrical identification of a subject in a relation of answerability. In the broadest outlines of the basic themes and conflicts that structure his novel (such as the opposition of principles of freedom, autonomy, and independence to principles of responsibility and answerability), in solutions to specific problems such as that of servitude, in the imagery of the transcendence of the face, in the diagnosis of the ethical dilemmas of his age, the solutions he proposes, and the very manner of formulating these solutions—Dostoevsky, through the character Zosima, frames and heralds some of Levinas's most creative, striking, and provocative formulas.

LUCE IRIGARAY

What Other Are We Talking About?

It is through misunderstanding or misjudgment that some people consider me a disciple or inheritor of Levinas's work. To be sure, there are some troubling similarities between our texts, notably in the use of words—similarities whose coherence I cannot always locate in Levinas's work as a whole, and which at times appear to me like grafts rather than natural outgrowths of his argumentation, of his language. This makes them barely intelligible to me, not for reasons of difficulty, I believe, but due to the temporal unfolding of his discourse. It is as though to an initial statement had later been added comments or clarifications or, indeed, corrections that are not easily integrated and would require moving to another stage of thought. This problem is perhaps particularly crucial in *Time and the Other*, a collection of lectures given in 1946 and 1947 and published by Fata Morgana in 1979. Although the preface asserts that this collection "reproduces the stenographic record" of the lectures and that the "spoken . . . style of this writing will surely be, for many, abrupt or awkward in certain turns of phrase" (*TO*, 29–30), I would point out that the preface also introduces the texts in terms rather different from those figuring in the body of the chapters, notably with regard to points that interest me and that I address in this essay. But I also find these rifts in the argument even within the volume, indeed within a single lecture. And I wonder what makes them possible, or justifies them philosophically.

Be that as it may, I have approached the question of the other along an entirely different path. And although our culture would certainly have benefited from a dialogue between our two perspectives, masculine and feminine, it stands only to lose from their assimilation. The real of the other as other would again be annulled, submerged in a single discourse—a discourse that remains egocentric and monological

YFS 104, *Encounters with Levinas,* ed. Thomas Trezise, © 2004 by Yale University.

even if it presents itself as anonymous or neuter, and that does not afford the other an irreducible existence, freedom, or speech. To conflate or even compare my words concerning the other with those of Levinas means once again to reduce the duality of subjects and of their differences, to include my thinking in Levinas's "virile" universe, where it cannot but lose its meaning and waste away.

I have sought dialogue with Levinas: through the reading of certain of his texts and through an invitation for exchange on the occasion of the publication of "The Fecundity of the Caress."[1] Each time, it was a failure—perhaps the kind of which Levinas speaks with regard to the difficult coexistence of two freedoms, and even the impossible communication between them? It is true that this question asserted or reasserted itself not long ago as one of those that our tradition, in particular our philosophical tradition, has excluded from its horizon. Whence the poverty of its teachings regarding relations between subjects, and especially between two subjects respectful of their mutual differences.

The differences that our culture has begun to integrate into its horizon have been, for a little more than a century, in some way quantitatively measurable in relation to the universe of a single subject alleged to represent the norm—differences pertaining, for example, to the insane, the worker, the foreigner, the child. The very relativity of these differences has not compelled us to recognize that different subjects belonging to different worlds exist. This forces us to leave the horizon of Western culture alone in order to glimpse the possible existence of an other culture, a culture in which the subject is no longer one and unique but two. Our logic is completely shaken by this—which is what I began to state and practice starting with *Speculum*, the subtitle of the book being: "On the Other as Woman."[2] In my view, there can in fact be no real recognition of the other as other unless the feminine subject is recognized as radically other with respect to the masculine subject, whatever their secondary resemblances or shared group membership. For lack of this gesture, the other is again reduced to a category of one and the same world, and to the possibility for a single subject to maintain, thanks to the category of "alterity," the permanence and development of that world.

Such a conception of the other subsists in Levinas's work. What does

---

1. In Luce Irigaray, *An Ethics of Sexual Difference*, trans. Carolyn Burke and Gillian C. Gill (Ithaca: Cornell University Press, 1993).

2. Irigaray, *Speculum of the Other Woman*, trans. Gillian C. Gill (Ithaca: Cornell University Press, 1985).

not exist in his work is the recognition of, and interaction between, two different subjectivities. While he attempts to avoid certain traps in the relation with the other, he still does not recognize that the other—beginning with a subject in the feminine—lives in a world other than his. And that what he experiences or says of it concerns his own universe.

The failure to appreciate the importance of the constitution of a world proper to the subject still entails today a failure to appreciate the importance of the difference between masculine and feminine subject, to the benefit of the difference between us and the foreigner: he or she who lives in a world more visibly outside our own, who belongs to a tradition or culture other than ours. Such a difference is certainly important but it is less decisive in the elaboration of subjectivity and of culture than the difference between the two kinds of the human species. It is also less universal and cannot moreover be treated outside of the gendered[3]—and not simply sexual—dimensions from which the relationships of union and filiation that characterize a tradition are constructed.

The traditional issues concerning the difference between man and woman, men and women, are obviously not reducible to the sole sphere of intimacy and eroticism, however important these may be. These issues are what structures a society or community, from the most subjective to the most objective, from the most singular to the most global aspect of its organization. They constitute the point from which a horizon can be reopened, without war or recidivism, and another society or culture can be built—provided they are considered with all the seriousness they deserve and a suitable method for approaching them is discerned.

In my view, the method here cannot be limited to a phenomenological approach, even if this approach remains pertinent. It is important, for example, to appeal to a more dialectical method, especially in order to account for that which, in subjectivity but also in the gendered relation, does not appear, does not present itself as a phenomenon. This is not only the case for the invisible, but also for other perceptions, no-

---

3. The term used by Irigaray is "sexué" ("dimensions sexuées"). "Sexué" commonly means reproductively sexual as opposed to asexual; hence its customary meaning is too narrow to convey a dimension that *includes* the "sexual" in a sense that, itself, is already wider than that of reproduction. We have chosen therefore to render "sexué" by "gendered"—but wish to emphasize that, if "gendered" is semantically more extensive than and irreducible to "sexual," it does not here mean "purely constructed" and is not opposed to "sexual" as culture might be opposed to nature.—Ed.

tably mental ones. It is therefore necessary to call anew on the negative, but in a manner different from that of Hegel. The negative will remain insurmountable, and it will serve to maintain the singularity of the subjectivity of the one and the other as well as the inalienability of the relation between the one and the other by the one or the other, or by any third party.

I will try to outline the need for such an approach with regard to the last chapters of *Time and the Other,* one of the texts in which I hoped, when writing *Speculum,* to find a theoretical complicity and the possibility of a dialogue with Levinas. But this expectation was already disappointed at that time. For Levinas, the other is ultimately not the other-woman, but the son, the one of whom he is not the owner, he says, but who he "is" (*TO,* 91). This return to genealogy, with its natural and hierarchical dimension, that is, to the most traditional aspect of the relationship between men in Western patriarchal culture, has seemed to me to be the result of the failure in the relation to the other as other of which Levinas speaks in the chapter devoted to "Eros." It also shows that vis-à-vis the other, Levinas is still situated in a relation to the same, and that, defined by a "category" of his world, namely, "alterity," the other as other has in this world no possibility of being or site to exist.

In Levinas's argument, an intersubjective dialectic between the two existents, masculine and feminine, is lacking; but also lacking is an intrasubjective dialectic between activity and passivity, for example, which a letting be of both myself and the other would allow, a letting be indispensable to the preservation and respect of the two [*du deux*] in the relation. Thus, a dialectic different from Hegel's is introduced without neglecting its teaching. The negative, applied by Hegel to that which is exterior to me, no longer serves as a way to integrate this exteriority into my world, to appropriate it, but rather to mark my limits as well as its own, and to create a between-two safeguarding the irreducibility of the two and protecting the relation from fusion, assimilation, or appropriation.

The horizon of a "total reciprocity" between the two, and therefore of a possibility for the two to be "interchangeable" (*TO,* 83), amounts to a nullification of the two that makes the relation to the other impossible. But it is also so in cases where the other is "the weak, the poor, 'the widow and the orphan'" while I am "the rich or the powerful" (*TO,* 83). In fact, the two are then submitted to a single measurement that could, sooner or later, render them interchangeable. We remain here in the domain of intra-subjectivity, in the sense that we remain within the horizon of a world pertaining to a single subject, a horizon within which this subject can alternatively become, according to space and time, weak or powerful, poor or rich.

A difference resists this possible alternation: sexual difference, or rather, gendered difference. A difference that presupposes a dialectic and an equilibrium between "justice" and "charity" (*TO*, 84) in a mode other than that evoked by Levinas. Justice here demands an equivalence and not an equality of rights, the latter implying a masked "preference" ordering the standardization of the rights that ought to maintain the duality of subjects and of their universes, while the former makes love possible. A love which can then include a reciprocity that will never be a reciprocating and which, thanks to this, can assure a future for the relation.

Levinas does not consider each term of a relation as belonging to a different world. He thus annuls the duality in the relation. This is apparent again in the subsequent chapters, such as the one devoted to eros. "Is there not a situation," writes Levinas, "where alterity would be borne by a being in a positive sense, as essence? What is the alterity that does not purely and simply enter into the opposition of two species of the same genus? I think the absolutely contrary contrary, whose contrariety is in no way affected by the relation that can be established between it and its correlative, the contrariety that permits its term to remain absolutely other, is the *feminine*" (*TO*, 85). The feminine is not other in "essence." This way of defining it bears witness to the masculine egocentrism of the culture in which such a statement is expressed. If the feminine is other for the masculine subject, the masculine is, or should be, also an other for the feminine subject. Levinas speaks of an "alterity that does not purely and simply enter into the opposition of two species [*espèces*] of the same genus [*genre*]." Why not: the opposition of two kinds [*genres*] of a single species [*espèce*]?[4] Continuing the commentary on this passage, in particular concerning the

---

4. Since, in taxonomy, a genus [*genre*] is more extensive than a species [*espèce*], translating "deux genres d'une même espèce" as "two genuses of a single species" would only lead to confusion. But since, on the other hand, in the quote from Levinas, taxonomy is not articulated verbatim by genre or sex, translating "genre" as "gender" will not do either. We have therefore chosen, in this context (and following its most common sense), to render "genre" as "kind."—Ed.

problem of the "contrary" and of "contrariety," I would emphasize the fact that difference, in particular sexual or more generally gendered difference, is in no way a contrariety and that defining the feminine as that which permits the term "to remain absolutely other" comes down to defining it on the basis of the masculine subject alone, which forgets the fact that it is itself other for this other for it which is the feminine.

Further proof that Levinas's remarks are situated within a single and unique world: "The difference between the sexes is a formal structure" (*TO*, 85). Now, this difference can only be understood in this way if it is envisioned within the horizon of the logic that Levinas claims to denounce. And while "the unity of Being proclaimed by Parmenides" can be interpreted on the basis of sexual difference—which Parmenides himself did, moreover, in proclaiming the importance of the Goddess in the constitution of Being—it does not "condition the very possibility of reality as multiple" (*TO*, 85). It is because sexual difference corresponds to an irreducibly dual real that it calls the unicity of Being into question—Being is two. The multiple goes well with the logic of the one—or the One—and even postulates it: the two belong to, are the two sides of, the same economy. No free space is provided between the one and the other—it is all already occupied, preoccupied. No place remains available to permit an encounter between two who do not simply form a whole, even if the duality of kinds constitutes the unity of the human species. There is a pre-given, natural unity, but whose accomplishment between two subjects escapes, is still and always to be constructed, and cannot be won through a complementarity, since duality would thereby be annulled. The whole that the duality of human kinds represents is stranger. While they can be one in the begetting of a child, it is very rare that man and woman succeed in creating between them a single energy, except in some fleeting ecstasy of desire. Duality allows them to distance themselves from each other as much as it allows them to unite to the point of being one. And the "fusion" of which Levinas speaks is above all a genealogical effect, the trace of an unresolved relationship with the maternal origin, and not the result of a relational becoming between autonomous adults of different kinds.

Between them, the negative at work is not equivalent to a nothingness: it is that which accounts for the alterity of the other and which protects it, like an inalienable good in some single absolute. It is what maintains the two and a non-unilateral relation between the two. And which does not require that the feminine be "essentially other" unless the masculine is also, but differently, for the feminine. But can alterity correspond to an essence? And is it not rather Being itself that reveals itself to be dual regarding the sexes, rendering their relation irreducible to appropriation in any form of oneness? Thenceforth, "profanation" (*TO*, 86), which is one of the intentional modalities of appropriation claimed by Levinas, appears useless. The relation to the mystery of the other demands, rather, a withdrawal that allows it to manifest itself, a listening to its alterity. An alterity that "hides from the light" (*TO*, 87), no doubt differently for a man and a woman. It is not in itself that the other remains invisible. It is invisible for me insofar as I cannot perceive the world in which it stands, or lives. It is invisible also, or at the same time, because of an interiority that does not give itself to be seen except indirectly, an interiority whose other name could be subjectivity, which is differently constituted for a man and a woman. If "the feminine is in existence an event different from that of spatial transcendence or of expression, which go toward the light" (*TO*, 87), one could say as much about the masculine subject capable of interiority. To claim that "hiding is the way of existing of the feminine" and that "this fact of hiding is precisely modesty" (*TO*, 87) reduces the feminine subject to an ontology determined by the needs of the masculine subject. And, if "this feminine alterity does not consist in the simple exteriority of an object," if "it is not made up either of an opposition of wills" (*TO*, 87), then it is not out of the question that the feminine corresponds, according to Levinas, to a dimension of interiority with which the masculine subject has not managed to endow itself and which it projects onto the other in order not to feel its lack and his own frustration. Without wondering for all that about the lack or frustration the feminine subject experiences due to this want of interiority in man— at least of an interiority not constructed by learned external models but corresponding to the cultivation by man of what he himself is. A cultivation whereby this "himself" would become capable of self-restraint or withdrawal, without the uncontrolled manifestation of drives or instincts depriving the other of an encounter with a world, a soul, or a spirit different from her own.

The man capable of withdrawing into himself also hides from the light, and his alterity also manifests itself through a withdrawal. The alterity of which Levinas speaks with regard to the feminine seems a bit too unilaterally tied to sex itself and to the economy of the sexual in the West—man being he whose sex exists in showing itself and woman being she whose sex exists in hiding itself. Of course, such a perspective appears preferable to that of existing or not existing, even if it is not unconnected to it. The subjectivity of the one and the other cannot however be constructed from this lone feature, nor can their difference be reduced to it, unless the masculine and the feminine are brought back to a double polarity within a single economy: the economy that the masculine subject has privileged in Western culture. The feminine within this economy is thought on the basis of the needs or desires of the masculine subject and not on its own basis. The two [*le deux*] therefore does not exist. The freedom of the one and the other does not subsist either, since this would amount to "the failure of communication" (*TO*, 87), according to Levinas. In my view, on the contrary, it amounts to the possibility of communication, provided the latter is understood as dialogue or intercommunication and not as the transmission of information or as tautologies within a single truth, a single world. The coexistence of two freedoms seems impossible for Levinas unless, as in Hegel, it is in the form of a struggle. "I do not initially posit the other as freedom" (*TO*, 87), writes Levinas. Personally, I would say that respecting the other as other comes down to initially recognizing it as free, that is, as being responsible for its becoming and its world, for its becoming as world. In Levinas's work, the other seems to be assimilated to a category within the world of a single subject. For me, the other exists as other on the basis of the existence of two different worlds. And it cannot be a question, for a subject, of "positing" the other or "the other's alterity" (*TO*, 87), except secondarily, as a "category" in its own world. I have rather to let the other be, to let it become or grow in keeping with a freedom that is certainly not identical to mine—in which case we would no longer be two—but equivalent to mine. Positing "alterity" as the "essence of the other"—necessarily a form of alienation for me (*TO*, 87)—amounts to enclosing the other within a category, or a dwelling, defined by me, and to preventing the coming of the other as event, or advent, irreducible in its freedom to my own world.

The event of a coming of the other does not occur "in the absolutely original relationship of eros"—a "relationship that is impossible to translate into powers" (*TO*, 88), writes Levinas, even though it can be analyzed as the source of many powers, perhaps still unrecognized by the philosopher and most men. Rather, it seems to be originally tied to the gendered—and not just the sexual—difference between subjects. Here is where the other appears to be most irreducibly other, a stranger to my own world. And not only because my desire goes toward him, or her, insofar as the other escapes my mastery, but because our subjectivities are differently constituted, and I aspire to the beyond of the world in which I dwell.

This difference is particularly obvious in the discourses produced by girls and boys, women and men. On this issue, I can only refer the reader to the research bibliography accompanying the text entitled "Le partage de la parole."[5] The specific relation that the masculine subject or the feminine subject maintains with him- or herself, with the world, with the other or others, but also with space and time, a relation to which their respective languages bear witness, entails the constitution of a world proper to each gender.

According to Levinas, alterity is a "category" corresponding to "an event in existing" that differs from "the hypostasis by which an existent arises" (*TO*, 88). In my view, the alterity of the other accompanies, and results from, the arrival of the other as other and as existent. The encounter with the other as other represents an event for the subjectivity and consciousness of each. And it is not without surprise that I read that "alterity is accomplished in the feminine. This term is on the same level as, but in meaning opposed to, consciousness" (*TO*, 88). Levinas has insisted a good deal on the fact that the alterity of the feminine "does not purely and simply enter into the opposition of two species of the same genus" (*TO*, 85). It is, however, in terms of an "opposed meaning" that he now argues. The feminine, "in meaning opposed to consciousness," "is not accomplished as a *being* [*étant*] in a transcendence toward light, but in modesty" (*TO*, 88).

I would have liked to ask Levinas of what light he is speaking here, if my proposals for dialogue on the occasion of the publication of "The Fecundity of the Caress" had not come up against these few words written in response: "I cannot agree with you." Différence sexuelle oblige? If the light evoked here by Levinas corresponds to the so-called natural light of Western reason, how could the feminine not stand back from it, since we know that it is founded through the exclusion of the feminine from its logic—be it as nature, as her or Her? It suffices to reread the philosophers, in particular the pre-Socratics, to be convinced of this and to follow the evolution of such a process.

But if the feminine is excluded from a certain light, from a certain consciousness, it does not amount for all that to a term of "opposed" or "inverse" meaning, except perhaps in the eyes of the masculine sub-

5. In Irigaray, *Le partage de la parole* (Oxford: European Humanities Research Centre, Special Lectures Series 4, 2001).

ject who has more or less deliberately so decided, notably by reducing the work of the negative to pairs of opposites. Relegating the feminine to the shadows, not even inviting it to participate in his light, man, in our tradition, has more or less explicitly constituted the feminine as the pole opposed to his becoming. Both resistance and reserve in relation to his project? But in this case it is still only a question of a consciousness in the masculine, or at least a Western consciousness. Nothing yet has been said of a consciousness in the feminine nor of its relation to the transcendental and to light. Why? Because the feminine is here considered only as what is at stake in masculine eros and not as a possible other subjectivity, inhabiting another world, a stranger to the one proper to the masculine subject. Only in this case does the feminine truly correspond to the other understood in the most original and universal sense. But it cannot for all this—or for this reason—be reduced to a category of a masculine form of logic: alterity. The feminine signifies the existence of a universe different from that of the masculine subject, structured according to other necessities, in particular relational ones, and another logic, including with regard to "spatial transcendence" and "light" (*TO*, 87). And it is not possible to define it as a "flight before light" (*TO*, 87). Perhaps it would be more correct to say that the feminine is not satisfied with the light sought by the masculine subject, that it aspires to another light, although it could share in the first through learning. But this light does not correspond to its constitutive necessities. And what the "feminine" tries to escape is rather the fact of being submitted to an economy not its own while its own goes unrecognized. The violation with respect to the feminine is firstly the imposition of a world inappropriate to it, which deprives it of a return to self, especially in the relation to the transcendental and to light.

And if Levinas sees no possibility other than to designate the feminine as "mystery," it is still from the point of view of the masculine universe that this property, indeed this "essence," is attributed to it. What is missing here is this: the feminine is a "mystery" for me (man), as and otherwise than I am a mystery for the feminine if I exist or am what I am. Each sex or gender is a mystery for the other, provided this other is not imprisoned in a category of one's own logic—alterity, for example. The other is a mystery for me insofar as it inhabits a world of its own, a world that is and will always remain strange to me if I respect the other as other. But, in order to communicate with this other—be it a he or a she—new means of communication are called for: communi-

cating with the other is impossible within a single logic. This is particularly true concerning the other as woman. Whence her inclusion in
or submission to the masculine world?

In order to attain to the respect of the other as other, beginning with
the other as woman, masculine subjectivity must recognize that its
world has limits beyond which the other lives. The other cannot be included within the boundaries of one's own universe—he, or she, stands
beyond, where I will never accede—which is not to say that I cannot
communicate with this world, thanks in particular to an insurmountable negativity taking into account the irreducibility of our difference.
And this not only in eros but in the relation with the other, from the
most everyday to the most universal, from the most natural of needs to
the most subtle aspect of the transcendental.

When Levinas links his category of alterity with eros, "with mystery, that is, with the future" (TO, 88), he seems to want to preserve the
possibility of a future, in particular for his desire, but not the reality of
the inalienability of the other to his world, in his world. For this other
belongs not only to the future of the subject but to its present, and also
to a past in which the other has never been recognized as such. In fact,
the other as other "can not be there [peut ne pas être là] when everything is there" (TO, 88), and this is how it marks the limit of a world
apprehended as a whole. To say that it is a question of a "category"—
"alterity"—and not of this—in particular this feminine—other present here next to me amounts to integrating this other into one's own
world. An empty slot [une case vide]—alterity—makes room for the
other in a logic foreign to it and in which it receives hospitality, provided it gives to this logic the wherewithal to continue functioning.
The empty slot is not equivalent to the exercise of an insurmountable
negativity, but rather to its avoidance and to the subsistence of a single
and fundamentally unchanged world. In this world, love is not "without reason" (TO, 88–89): it seeks an opening, a future, for a closed universe.

Thus is explained what Levinas writes on the caress: that it belongs
to the world of light (read: his light), that "what is caressed is not
touched, properly speaking," and that "the caress does not know what
it seeks," which constitutes its "essence" (TO, 89). Eros would then be
the "not knowing" to which Levinas grants a place in his economy in
order to maintain a breach, "a game with something slipping away, a
game absolutely without project or plan, not with what can become

ours or us, but with something other, always other, always inaccessible, and always still to come. The caress is the anticipation of this pure future, without content" (*TO*, 89).

Levinas's caress stays firmly within, at best at the edge, of his world, seeking what could erode its closure toward a future not included in the past and the present. To be sure, it testifies to a desire to leave the prison of tautology, but not for all that to a desire to communicate with the other. It "plays" with the "not knowing" of "something other" without being on the way toward someone other. It even uses this other, especially this feminine other, in its own universe in order to create in it "the anticipation of this pure future, without content." This feminine other whom Levinas caresses is what will give "a horizon of the future" to his world, "a horizon where a personal life can be constituted" thanks to "the absence of the other" (*TO*, 90). The other is, is only, the empty slot that causes communication to fail and creates time for the subject. The other is that which assures the subject of a "victory over death" (*TO*, 90), on condition that it not be there, that it never be present—a failure to seize, and thus the enclosure of the subject thanks to this absence, but without any recognition of the other's own existence.

Levinas's concern is to avoid "fusion" or "possession" in eros. However, the use that he makes of the other, including in the caress, seems to be a very subtle, I would say spiritual, even transcendental, appropriation of the other. Although he tries to avoid two traps in the relation with the other, his remarks here do not allude to a being with the other. Being with the other cannot be reduced to "fusion," "possession," or "knowledge," because the two [*le deux*] would thereby be annihilated. Being with the other supposes the passage to another way of communicating, where light and transcendence are both shared and preserved in their singularity.

Levinas does not inquire about the possibility of this different economy, neither the "contrary" nor the "inverse" of his, which would still mean envisaging it on the basis of one and the same world. The alterity of the feminine is envisaged by him as a kind of antiworld in the debate that the philosopher probably carries on with the maternal universe without recognizing the existence of a feminine world irreducible to his—a world with which fusion is impossible short of exiling the feminine from the site proper to it. This is, however, what Levinas attempts to do, as he explains in "Phenomenology of Eros" (*TI*, 256–66) but also in the chapter of *Time and the Other* on eros. Indeed, functioning for the philosopher only as an "increase of hunger, of ever richer promises, opening new perspectives onto the ungraspable," the "intentionality of the voluptuous—the sole intentionality of the future itself" is not an "expectation of some future fact"—an encounter with the other (*TO*, 89). The autoeroticism here at work is at the service of the philosophical, of spirituality in the masculine, indeed of a God in the masculine, but it is not recognized as such by those who give themselves up to it in order to give themselves some time, without worrying about the disposition of a shared space or time. Thus the caress can bring back the other, woman, to "childhood" or "animality"—therefore outside of human space-time—while man will have used it in order to continue his search for transcendence, be it philosophical or religious.

If the avoidance of "fusion," "possession," or "knowledge" in eros results in relegating one to animality and the other to the search for a transcendental horizon of its own, what human coexistence is possible between the two? Belonging to what species, kingdom, or genus?

The evanescence of pleasure in the opening to a future is not as sublime as it seems here. For a "content" has been neglected: the existence of the other and the obligation to look for the path of a being-with that is human for everyone, and not torn between the poles of animality and divinity in a single subjective economy. The failure of eros is to be found here: in the absence of the construction of a being-with-the-other. It is the failure of the trajectory of Western man, which has engendered many "powers," "fusions," and "possessions"—sometimes obvious, sometimes so subtle as to seem sublime. Thus, the most sublime aspect of eros lies in seeking the revival of one's desire, thereby opening a future of one's own, without ever abandoning oneself to the other or with the other in the ungraspable transcendence of a between-two.

Levinas confirms this failure in the subsequent chapter. For, although he refuses "fusion" and "possession," he wonders: "How, in the alterity of a you, can I remain I, without being absorbed or losing myself in that you? How can the ego that I am remain myself in a you, without being nonetheless the ego that I am in my present, that is, an ego that inevitably returns to itself? How can the ego become other to itself? This can happen only in one way: through paternity" (*TO*, 91). Levinas makes the feminine bear this alteration of the self that the voluptuous entails, but he challenges it for himself. He doubtless fears losing his ego in it. Or he fears entrusting the safeguard of his ego to the feminine? It is in the son that he ultimately finds the prototype of his other:

"Paternity is the relationship with a stranger who, while being other, is myself, the relationship of the ego with a myself who is nonetheless a stranger to me" (*TO*, 91). The other is therefore a very part of or participation in me. Of course, I am not its owner, I do not have it, but I "am" it (*TO*, 91).

Levinas goes on to specify that "the son is not some event that happens to me—for example, my sadness, my ordeal, or my suffering" (*TO*, 91). And even my voluptuousness? The son is "an ego, a person" (*TO*, 91). Whose place is prepared by the transcendence of the temporal horizon opened by the absence of the other, woman, in eros? It is he, the son, who guarantees "the father's exteriority" and "a pluralist existing" (*TO*, 92). Resolving, indeed annulling in a way, the relational problems posed by the difference in the duality of the sexes? But the son would not be possible without this difference.

Levinas has little concern for the "ego" of the mother, present in the "son," or for the fecundity of the father in the begetting of the daughter. Although he asserts the "ontological value" of the "fecundity of the ego" in paternity—while saying it is a question of a "biological category" (*TO*, 92)—it seems that, for him, sexual difference does not deserve such a status. Now, in my view, sexual difference concerns the ontological dimensions much more radically, allowing the problematic of Being to be maintained outside of any essentialism provided that its unicity, its world, and its values are doubled. This leads one to enter into an entirely different logic, an entirely different dialectic concerning the horizon of temporality and of alterity. Here, fecundity and begetting no longer necessarily pertain to a "biological category," but will first have a spiritual value. Provided there are two to beget, two different ones engendering not only the son, a third party as it were, but themselves and their work thanks to the fecundity of the strangeness of their worlds for each other.

It is surprising that, in reference to the event of the arrival of the other, Levinas speaks of "ego" [*moi*] and not of "I" [*je*] in these pages. Could this be the result of reducing the world of the subject to an ego, forgetful of all the interrelational ties that bind it to a world? In the encounter or being with the other, it is rather above all a question of "I," and of an irreducibly dual "I," finding itself present in the present [*en présence au présent*]. A present that is therefore a place of encounter with the other: not only a "tear in the infinite beginningless and endless fabric of existing" (*TO*, 52), but the possibility of accomplishment of this existing or relational being which is the human. A "hypostasis," no doubt, in relation to an existing that supposes or believes itself to be solitary, but a hypostasis always already included in this existing as the event opening the impersonality or the anonymity of a "one" or a "there is" through a being-with-the other existing from the beginning, within and without.

This being-with-the-other is misunderstood, forgotten, neglected in its hypostasis at work in and outside of my flesh, of my subjectivity. No Other could insure its substitution. At best, the hypostasis of time is kept open, so that a path leading or leading back toward the other can be sought, as well as the mediations or means to be able to be with him, or her, present in the present. Leaving the space between us open. Interlacing in the construction of the work of being-with-the-other, with respect for our difference or differences, horizontal and vertical transcendence, without one ever being able to exclude the other. Which allows us, even obliges us, to take into account both the one and the other, to incarnate the one and the other, in us and between us—not without limits, but without end. The temporal horizon is thus kept indefinitely open for the one, for the other, and for the between-two of the relation. Such a gesture is no longer dependent on a morality more or less paternalistic with regard to the other—understood as "the weak, the poor, 'the widow and the orphan,'" indeed the "son"—but on the cultivation of a reciprocal desire between two different existents and Beings.

—Translated by Esther Marion

PAUL RICOEUR

Otherwise:
A Reading of Emmanuel Levinas's
Otherwise than Being or
Beyond Essence[1]

OTHERWISE THAN . . . :
Saying and the Said

This study is motivated by the desire to understand Levinas at his most difficult. This desire explains the choice of *Otherwise than Being or Beyond Essence* as the almost exclusive guide to my reading. The greatest gamble undertaken by this book is that of linking the fate of the relation to be established between the ethics of responsibility and ontology to the fate of their respective languages: *Saying* on the side of ethics, the *said* on the side of ontology.[2] It is a bold gamble to the extent that what binds each of these disciplines to its own manner of signifying brings to the fore two difficulties generated by this new way of philosophizing: on the one hand, the difficulty, for ethics, of freeing itself from its ceaseless confrontation with ontology; on the other, the difficulty of finding for the ex-ception that disrupts the system of being, the language appropriate to it, its *own* language, the *said* of its *Saying*. These difficulties are inseparable and are condensed in the word, the adverb *otherwise, otherwise than*. . . .It is, indeed, always necessary to tear oneself away, through the *otherwise than* . . . , from the very thing whose reign one attempts to suspend or interrupt; but at the same time, some linguistic articulation must be ventured for that *in the name of which* one is conscripted and assured of being able, of having, to pronounce the anteriority of the ethics of responsibility with respect to the "rhythm [*train*] of being, the rhythm of essence" (though a note on the

1. This essay appeared in French as *Autrement: Lecture d'*Autrement qu'être ou au-delà de l'essence *d'Emmanuel Levinas* (Paris: Presses Universitaires de France, 1997).
2. Both Levinas and Ricoeur are inconsistent in their capitalization of "saying" and "said." We follow, respectively, their original texts in the translation.—Ed.

YFS 104, *Encounters with Levinas*, ed. Thomas Trezise, © 2004 by Yale University.

first page points out that one should really write "essance," with an "a"). In the background of these twin difficulties, I would like to bring out a difficulty that is not formulated as such, namely, the overlapping of the system of Saying and the ethics of responsibility.

Two preliminary remarks.

First, the book neither offers nor allows for any introduction. One plunges immediately *in medias res,* as with Hegel denying the possibility of an introduction to philosophy that would not already itself be philosophy, and as with Heidegger, whose declaration that the question of being has been forgotten, in the first line of the first page of *Being and Time,* amounts to the erasure of any preface.

The second remark is bound to the first: there is no noticeable progression in Levinas's argument; the successive chapters are not added one to the other; everything is said in the section entitled "The Argument" (*OB,* 1–20) and, in a way, repeated in the brief final pages, which bear a title of particular interest for us here: "Otherwise Said." That which is otherwise than the said of Saying seeks for itself—and perhaps gives itself—an *otherwise said.* Between these two extremes stretches what, at the end of "The Argument" (*OB,* 19), the author calls "The Itinerary"—a word immediately glossed by the term *ex-position* (which in turn becomes the title of Chapter II). This word announces not so much a step beyond "The Argument" (which, in a sense, is complete) as an unfurling, an *unfolding* [*dépli*] that reveals the major fold [*pli*] of the ethics of responsibility, that is, *substitution,* "substitution as the *otherwise than being* at the basis of proximity" (*OB,* 19). So, an unfolding, or a delving, if you prefer, which *on the level of discourse,* and because of the kind of discourse employed in this book, poses the question of *thematization* in a philosophy that, as we shall see, places themes, thematics, and thematization on the side of the *said.* If therefore any advance were possible within such a philosophy, it would consist in showing the derivation of the discourse of ontology from the discourse of ethics, a derivation that is repeatedly announced and actually begun with the notions of *the third party* and of *justice* as keynotes. The place these notions occupy with respect to substitution and its one-in-the-place-of-the-other creates a difficulty in its turn. I will save for the second part of my study the thematics of the third party and of justice, which may be termed an advance inasmuch as it brings forth a new *said* occasioned by the *Saying* otherwise than *said*—the very one that the last chapter of Levinas's book terms precisely the *otherwise said.*

Let us, then, enter into "The Argument," which will be filled in within the unfolding of the folds that constitute the remainder of the book.

"The Argument" begins in a frank manner with the first subtitle: "Being's 'Other' " (*OB*, 3). This subtitle says everything or rather *unsays everything*, the all, totality. The fundamental opposition so announced is meant to dissociate the otherwise than being from all other figures of the other, which, as will be shown, ontology includes, absorbs or, as is frequently said, "recuperates." "Being's essence dominates notbeing itself" (*OB*, 3). The *otherwise than . . .* transcends the *other* who, in a way, circulates in the intervals of being's negativity and absorbs the internecine war into the peace of compensation. Now, one never has done with these figures of the other as intervals of nothingness that make of being an *inter-esse*, an interest [*intér-essement*]—which marks the triumph, and not the subversion, of being. This is when, without delay, the two protagonists of the drama that gives the book its substance take the stage: *Saying* and the *said.* All the cards are played in a single move: Saying, the verb to Say, joined to "proximity of the one to the other," to "disinterestedness [*désintéressement*]," to "responsibility of the one for the other," to "substitution." These key terms are gathered in a bouquet on a single page (*OB*, 6) where, as the author admits, he inquires "by anticipation."

But let us begin the unfolding. Why should *Saying,* the presumed language of the responsibility of the one for the other, be immediately termed "original" or even "pre-original"? And this, with respect to *what* origin, included in the ontological system of the said? Well, with respect to a linguistic *correlation* that annuls the otherwise of Saying to the benefit of the said. This correlation makes of Saying a simple internal division and ultimately subordinates Saying to the said: "The correlation of saying and the said, that is, the subordination of saying to the said, to the linguistic system and to ontology, is the price that manifestation demands" (*OB*, 6). Let us pause here: Levinas indicates that he does not expect anything from a distinction between Saying and the said that would remain a correlation and would not constitute an uprooting, a substitution, a "reduction" (in a non-Husserlian sense). This play, considered internal to the apophansis sufficient for a beingcentered philosophy, is the one that the analytic philosophy of language has systematized in the opposition between a propositional semantics and a pragmatics of utterance—terms in which one recognizes, respectively, the said and Saying. It is precisely this correlation that Levinas finds irrelevant, philosophically speaking. This first figure of the other constitutes no more, according to him, than an appendix, an out-growth, of propositional semiotics. Why so? Because *apophansis* tends toward nominalization, the name-making of all the resources of meaning in language. Levinas bases his argument here on the fact that the correlation Saying-said relies on the linguistic correlation between verb and noun. And this we have known since the Cratylus, which founds the predicative act upon the noun-verb (*onoma-rhēma*) polarity. In fact, two modern versions of this correlative structure confirm the *Cratylus:* in phenomenology, the couple noesis-noema; in linguistic theory, the assignation of verbs to events or actions, as in Davidson's *Essays on Actions and Events.* Whether it be a question of the phenomenology of noesis or the linguistics of the verb, both versions of the correlation between verb and noun opened up the possibility of a pragmatics of Saying that, at first glance, might justify a dialectics of Saying and the said. But for Levinas, this could be nothing more than a correlation that annuls alterity, as he tries to show in the analysis of predication, which he sees as a partial identification of the predicate with the subject—partial inasmuch as saying "A is B" is not saying "A is A." Nevertheless, it is an identification as long as one can derive denomination from predication through the assimilating "as," the famous *als was* to which Heidegger refers. Thus would identity labor beneath, in, and through difference. Predication, in this sense, remains an operation by which identity prevails over difference. This is an initial way in which to claim that there is no true difference, no true alterity, before the alterity of the other in its approach and proximity.

Does this close the debate? We shall see further on that, in the search for a signifying discourse appropriate to the discovery of responsibility, a certain revenge of the *name*—the proper name—will benefit a *said* posterior to the ethical reduction of the apophantic said.

Let us summarize this movement of thought before considering another temptation—or seduction—of alterity, to which the articulation of an *unsaying* will respond.

Levinas gathers under the rubric of the *thematic*, equivalent to the doxic thesis of phenomenology, a new correlative unity of Saying and the said, in which a certain usage of the category of the other comes to light, only to be neutralized. At this point we reach the origin of what I have called the "second difficulty" posed by the discourse of the author of *Otherwise than Being*, the difficulty of thematizing itself in turn and in its proper place as ex-ception, that is, the place, in the discourse of ethics, of the approach, of proximity, of responsibility, of sub-stitution. For the time being, the discourse can only be one of denun-ciation, in the sense in which one denounces a pact—a denunciation fed by an accusation of *betrayal.* I read: "We have been seeking the *oth-erwise than being* from the beginning, and as soon as it is conveyed be-fore us it is betrayed in the said that dominates the saying that states it" (*OB,* 7). It is indeed, if one dare say so, a betrayal of betrayal that Le-vinas expresses with the term "unsaying": "The *otherwise than being* is stated in a saying that must also be unsaid in order thus to extract the *otherwise than being* from the said in which it already comes to signify but a *being otherwise*" (*OB,* 7). One begins to see here what is at stake in this battle against all figures of alterity [*l'autre*] that would not be the other [*autrui*], that would be no more than variations of *being oth-erwise* and therefore betrayals of the *otherwise than being.* But will the otherwise than being find its said in the process of its unsaying? The whole methodology of the book is at stake in this.

But let us continue the work of unsaying. Without yet leaving the field of linguistics and logic, of the apophansis that Levinas denounces, let us focus on the prefix "pre-" in "pre-original" and the prefix "dia-" in "dia-chrony." First the "pre-" in "pre-original." The quarrel with lin-guistic theories that make of Saying an appendix of the said brings out a usage of the notion of origin that must also be rejected. Speech Act theory and even, on a more general level, a linguistics of sentences like Benveniste's, suggest that the speaking subject performs an *act* of say-ing and therefore takes the discursive initiative. This initiative tends to make of the speaking subject the origin of its Saying. This Levinas rejects out of hand since, in the "approach," the initiative comes as a matter of principle from the other [*l'autre*], others [*autrui*]. I personally see in this an extremely difficult problem. Is it permitted to strip Say-ing of its active character in order to make it compatible with the pas-sivity "more passive than all passivity" (*OB,* 15), the passivity per-taining to the reception of responsibility imposed on the self by the other? Whatever the case may be, we have touched here, at whatever cost, upon the reason for introducing into our discussion the "pre-" in "pre-original"—which entails the "an-" in "an-archy." The an-archy of ethical Saying eludes the *archē,* the origin [*archie*] of utterance, re-duced to a simple outgrowth of the apophantic said. But doesn't the pre-fix "pre-" signify temporal anteriority? Here the ontological other raises another of its hydra heads, which must in turn be lopped off. This is the assumed other of *temporal* anteriority. An assumed other, inasmuch as the "retained past" is recuperated by the present of presence. What is in question here is no longer simply the present of the initiative of utterance, but the present of presence in which, according to Levinas, Husserl absorbed, recovered the alterity of the past by means of "retention" and even more through the assimilation of retrospection to a synthesis of retentions of retentions. Here Levinas plays *proximity*, in the ethical sense, to its fullest against *anteriority* in its onticoontological sense. Levinas refuses the help that might have been afforded him in this respect by a phenomenology of memory, history, and narration. For him, these three operations *synchronize* what Saint Augustine yet called *distentio animi* (these are my words, but I believe that they follow the path laid out in Levinas's book). He argues indefatigably in favor of a *dia-chrony* devoid of any recuperative *synchrony*. He recognized no irreducible diachrony in memory or history, since the linguistic mediation of narrative neutralizes, according to him, the passage of time as dis-sociation, as dia-chrony. This head-on battle waged against history and memory is all the more significant in that Saint Augustine had translated as *distentio* the Neoplatonic *diastasis*. But, according to Levinas, this *diastasis* doe not involve an irrecuperable gap [*écart*] as do the approach and the proximity of the other. On this point there are numerous, though short and allusive, passages concerning the "recovery of all the gaps" constitutive of the dephasing of the instant with respect to itself that makes of time a *passing*, a gap-like lapse. Thus, he refers to time as "a recuperation of all gaps, through retention, memory, and history. In its temporalization, in which, through retention, memory, and history, nothing is lost, everything is presented or represented . . . everything is synthesized or, as Heidegger would say, gathered, in which everything is crystallized or sclerosed into substance—in recoverable temporalization, without time lost, without time to lose, and where the being of substance comes to pass—there must be signaled a lapse of time without return, a diachrony refractory to all synchronization, a transcendent diachrony" (*OB*, 9).

In this sense, the past as memorable, that is, rendered representable by memory and history, can be thematized. Whence the characterization of Saying not only as pre-original but as pre-memorable, breaking with synchronization. Here the prefix "pre-" is linked to the prefix "dia-" in "dia-chronic" ("a diachrony refractory to all synchronization"). But we must consider that this anteriority of a pre-original and an-archic *past* is not itself inscribed in the synchronizable time of memory and history. It is in this sense that it is immemorial (or better yet, immemorable). Here Levinas uses as an argument the Husserlian conception of the retention of retentions taken as a modification of the consciousness of the present. Perhaps Heideggerian *Wiederholung* should also be suspected of "synchronizing," in some way, the three temporal ekstases in a being-all [*être-tout*], as the title and the content of the last section of *Being and Time* suggest. It did not occur to Levinas that memory might be interpreted as the recognition of a temporal distance that is irrecuperable in re-presentation. But this would require freeing memory itself of any hold that re-presentation has on it. Otherwise, how could one write the poignant dedication: "To the memory of those who were closest . . ."? Is it not this memory, once it has undergone the test of alterity, loss, and mourning, that allows for the appearance of this "past not returning as a present" (*OB*, 10), or "the past that bypasses the present" (*OB*, 11), or again, "a past that never was present" (*OB*, 24)?

In our reconstruction of the discourse adopted in *Otherwise than Being*, we are faced with the obvious difficulty of matching the pre-originality of the discourse of Saying with the contemporaneity of the neighbor's *approach*. To be sure, the pre-original, in Levinas, is dechronologized and detemporalized as much as possible. But here is where I see a real difficulty: the affinity between the "dia-chrony refractory to all synchronization" and what I cannot think of, it seems, except as the contemporaneity of the approach, raises a question. And it is with this question that the ethical relation [*l'éthique*] is opened, or rather it is this question that opens the ethical relation.

I would like to see as the culmination of this struggle against the figures of the other that are purportedly recoverable in an ontology, the most radical figure of unsaying, that is, the one that is brought forth by the *ontological difference* between being and entities in Heidegger. It is important—and from this point of view, highly significant—that Levinas speaks of the ontological difference in terms of "amphibology," where this term is understood to mean a production of ambiguity, of equivocalness within a homogeneous conceptual field. With the difference between being and entities we are still under the reign of correlation, as we were with the difference between discourse and the said in apophantics. Of this amphibology it is asserted that it "does not signify the ultimate" (*OB*, 23). For that matter, the section entitled "The Amphibology of Being and Entities" (*OB*, 38–43) chases down the betrayal of Saying in an otherwise that is not at the level of the otherwise than being. Being is clearly otherwise than entities. But here the difference that attracts the ear is in fact nothing more than a doubling. If I should say "red reddens" (this brings to mind the Heideggerian expression "time temporalizes"), under the appearance of Saying, the verb remains caught up in the net of denomination: "The Said, as a verb, is the *essence* of *essence*" (*OB*, 39). *Essence* is the very fact that there is theme, ostension, *doxa* or *logos,* and thus truth. "Essence is not only conveyed, it is temporalized in a predicative statement" (*OB*, 39). The verbality of the verb does not create a true gap relative to the substantiality of the noun. The verb's "resonance" will only be recognized as such in the injunction to responsibility. One must admit that being, as verb, does not extract us from the said of the nominalized participle. In this sense, Heidegger's philosophy does not escape the "deafness as profound as that which hears only nouns in language" (*OB*, 41). It is striking that one should find in the section devoted to the amphibology of being and entities the most virulent pages against the capture of Saying in the said, as if this capture were in fact only thematized in the amphibology of being and entities. Such is amphibology: "To be thenceforth *designates* instead of *resounding*" (*OB*, 42). But Levinas does not feel that this is enough: at the end of this decisive section he attempts to give to this virulent unsaying the shape of a question.

The question, here, constitutes a temptation if not an actual betrayal: "We must," Levinas states, "go back to what is prior to this correlation [between Saying and the said]" (*OB*, 43). True enough, but the question remains: "Is *Saying* just the active form of the *Said*? Does '*saying itself*' amount to '*being said*' ['*Se dire*' revient-il à '*être dit*']?" (*OB*, 43). We can guess that the response is negative: *Saying itself* dissociates itself from being said when it signifies "to answer," "to offer oneself," "to suffer."

   This is where the Husserlian vocabulary of "reduction" (*OB*, 43–45) suggests itself as a recourse. The reduction of the reduction of Saying, if one dares say so, to the active form of the said. The uprooting, the liberation of Saying from the condition of "an echo of the reduced *Said*" (*OB*, 44). This liberation is accomplished only in the "*ethical interruption of essence*" (*OB*, 44, my emphasis). Then follows this admission: "But one can go back to this signification of Saying—responsibility and substitution—only from the Said and from the question: 'What about . . . ?' ['Qu'en est-il de . . . ?'], a question already internal to the Said in which everything shows itself" (*OB*, 44). I speak of admission: if, indeed, one can never have done with being otherwise, it is only where the solidity of dissimulating correlations is fissured that an echo of Saying makes itself heard in the said, promising the possibility of going back from the said to Saying. "But here," Levinas exclaims, "is the reduction of the said to Saying, beyond the Logos, beyond being and non-being—beyond essence, beyond the true and the not-true—the reduction to signification, to the one-for-the-other of responsibility (or more exactly of substitution) . . . " (*OB*, 45).

SAID OTHERWISE
The third party and justice

1—Proximity, responsibility, substitution

Let us reiterate the difficulty: how can one match the line of reasoning in "The Argument" for the irreducibility of Saying to the said with the discourse in the middle section of the work on proximity, the dissymmetrical relation of responsibility and, crowning the work, substitution? I would like to show that the disconcerting irruption of the theme of the third party and justice in several strategic locations in the book has something to do with this difficulty as well as, to anticipate, with the very possibility of the discourse adopted throughout the book *on* the equation of Saying, as discursive instance, and responsibility as the sovereign instance of an ethics without ontology.

The pages devoted to the triad of *proximity, responsibility*, and *substitution* are written in a tone that might be called declarative, if not kerygmatic, sustained by an insistent, if not obsessive, use of the trope of hyperbole. It is through these two traits, the tone and the trope, that I will characterize the production of Saying in ethics. But can this Saying do without a corresponding said? It is to the treatment of this question that, in my view, the position of the third party and of justice pertains.

Let us concentrate on Chapter III, entitled "Sensibility and Proximity," and Chapter IV, entitled "Substitution," which, according to the author, is the heart of the book and, as it were, its origin.

Extremes are quickly reached: proximity is called an "obsession"; with this sudden rupture, the difference of the same and the other becomes non-indifference. Saying comes about in the obsession with the neighbor. "Saying, in which the speaking subject is exposed to the other, is not reducible to the objectification of a stated theme. What then has come to wound the subject, so that it should expose its thoughts or expose itself in its Saying?!" (OB, 84). In order to say the affected being, one must say the exposed being—and in order to say the exposed being, one must say the attacked, wounded, traumatized being. Worse still, one must Say the accused in the accusative "me" [me]. We are indeed at the crossroads of the problematics of Saying and the ethical relation: "The proper signification of subjectivity is proximity, but proximity is the very signifyingness of signification, the very establishing of the one-for-the-other, the establishing of the sense that every thematized signification reflects in being" (OB, 85). Let us put aside the last part of that sentence for now, as it will lead us far from shore, in order to focus on signification and signifyingness in conjunction with proximity.

Obsession, wound, traumatism: why such extreme terms? Why this escalation of the pathic to the pathetic and the pathological? Because one is never finished with the opposite obsession, that of appearance, of phenomenality: "The neighbor as *other* does not allow itself to be preceded by any precursor who would depict or announce its silhouette. *It does not appear*" (OB, 86, my emphasis). The neighbor concerns me without appearing. It is this "without appearing" that one has never finished Saying. "Obsession is not consciousness, nor a species or a modality of consciousness" (OB, 87). Redundancy in denial. We must take full measure of the violence that is thus inflicted upon the very language of the face. One might be tempted to think that the other appears in its face, is given to be seen. Not at all: it escapes representation; it is "the very collapse of phenomenality" (OB, 88). Nor is there a shared present between the other and me, despite the naïve expectation expressed at the end of the first part of this study. The neighbor is not my contemporary; otherwise we should return to the synchrony with which, as we saw above, memory, history, and narration are burdened: "Proximity is a disturbance of rememberable time" (OB, 89). "One can call that apocalyptically the shattering of time. But it is a matter of the effaced but untameable diachrony of non-historical, non-said time, which cannot be synchronized in a present by memory and historiography, where the present is but the trace of an immemorial past. . . . Such is the sense of the non-phenomenality of the face" (OB, 89). It orders without showing itself, without making itself seen. "Exorbitance" against "conjunction." Only the charm of the caress, "a denuding never naked enough" (*OB*, 90), disrupts this extremism. How strangely beautiful are these pages that celebrate the beauty of the skin "with wrinkles, a trace of itself" (*OB*, 90)! But the hunt for the trace begins again, "trace of ex-cession, of the excessive" (*OB*, 91).

Ex-cession, the excessive, are concentrated in the movement from proximity to substitution, that is, from suffering *through* the other to suffering *for* the other. What more could substitution add—in excess—to proximity? What makes it the equivalent of "the very signifyingness of signification, which signifies in *Saying* before showing itself in the *Said*" (*OB*, 100)? In fact (and aside from the recapitulative nature of the work as a whole, which is due to its previous publication in parts and which it retains in its final form), this central chapter succeeds only in reinforcing the rupture effect already exerted by the vocabulary of inflicted wounds through recourse to an even more extreme vocabulary, that of persecution and hostage taking. The Self occupies the place of the other without having either chosen or wished to do so. The "despite oneself" of the hostage condition signifies the extreme passivity of the injunction. This paradox—of an inhumane condition called upon to say the ethical injunction—should be shocking. The non-ethical says the ethical solely by virtue of its excess. If substitution must signify something irreducible to a will to suffer, in which the Self would recover mastery over itself in the sovereign gesture of the offering, of oblation, then it must remain an "expulsion of self outside of itself . . . the self emptying itself of itself" (*OB*, 110–111). In short, it must be by its "very malice" that "persecuting hatred" (*OB*, 111) *signifies* the "subjection through the other" of the injunction under the aegis of the Good. I wonder whether Levinas's readers have assessed the enormity of the paradox that consists in having malice say the extreme degree of passivity in the ethical condition. It is "outrage," the height of injustice, that one asks to signify the call to benevolence: "It is through the condition of being hostage that there can be in the world pity, compassion, pardon, and proximity" (*OB*, 117). That is not all; the "trauma of persecution" (*OB*, 111) must also signify the "the irremissibility of accusation" (*OB*, 112), in short, limitless guilt. Here Dostoyevsky takes over from Isaiah, Job, and the Koheleth. Here we have a kind of crescendo: persecution, outrage, expiation, "absolute accusation, prior to freedom" (*OB*, 118). Does this not constitute an admission that an ethics disconnected from ontology has no direct, appropriate language of its own? This question puts us on the path of a reading hypothesis that will be proposed further on concerning the strategic role played by the theme of the third party in the discourse of the philosopher writing *Otherwise than Being.* The distress in the discourse is further exacerbated by the denial and rejection of any "theological, appeasing or consoling" solution. To the extent that a foundational or justificative function might be assigned to such a solution, Levinas's text is in this respect violently anti-theological. The desert of words: "The self as expiation is prior to activity and passivity" (*OB*, 116). It is not as a "capable" man—"'capable'" of expiating (*OB*, 118)—that the ego is solicited: "It is this original expiation. This expiation is involuntary, for it is prior to the will's initiative" (*OB*, 118). It is in this way that expiation is not redemption, inasmuch as redemption would reestablish equality, adequation, and commensurability, as in Hegelian forgiveness. Levinas does not want to be forgiven in that way, nor at that price. Nor does he wish to forgive.

Have we sufficiently shown that the Saying of responsibility cannot help but add, to the unsaying of any equalizing relation, a *revulsive tropology* extending from wound to outrage? A tropology of inflicted violence? Have we sufficiently shown that nothing is *said* about responsibility as a theme? That the saying of responsibility is exhausted in this crescendo of the discourse of malice?

2—The third party and justice

It is against this background of what I would dare to call *verbal terrorism* that the discourse of justice arises and is maintained on the terrain of the third party. How does one gain access to it? In the book and its discourse, furtively. Not once, but twenty, thirty times, and always as though in passing, in saying for no reason. Perhaps it is only belatedly [dans l'*après-coup*] that this thrust [*coup de force*] can acquire meaning. Here is the first occurrence of the theme—for it is indeed a theme, and the only one allowed in "The Argument" (*OB*, 1–20). In this text is announced what Plato would have called a "second navigation." "There must be a justice among incomparables. There must then be a comparison of incomparables and a synopsis, togetherness and contemporaneity; there must be thematization, thought, history, and inscription" (*OB*, 16). The question then arises of what legitimizes this apparent reversal. Levinas continues, after the text just quoted: "But being must be understood on the basis of *being's other.* To be on the basis of the signification of the approach is to be *with the other* for or against the third party, with the other and the third party against oneself" (*OB*, 16; note the use of "with" on the basis of the earlier "through" and "for" the other). And a bit further on: "In this disinterestedness [the subtitle of "The Argument" is "Essence and Disinterest"] . . . the justice that compares, assembles, and conceives, the synchrony of being and peace, take form" (*OB*, 16). At issue here is indeed a Said derived from Saying—a Said of "thought, justice, and being" (*OB*, 19). A Said that will be a "saying again" (*OB*, 20) amongst philosophers, a "saying again" that soon will allow for the reappropriation of the Platonic Good and the Cartesian Infinite. "It is through the *already said* that words, elements of a historically constituted vocabulary, will come to function as signs and acquire a use, and bring about the proliferation of all the possibilities of vocabulary" (*OB*, 37). The hypothesis becomes clearer: it is justice that allows one to *thematize* the type of Saying that allows one to philosophize. But from what position, what post shall one speak? From the position, the place of the third party, namely that other who is not the near but the far, the stranger, as in the Bible, as in Plato's *The Sophist*. "One should then also recall that proximity is not from the outset a juridical judgment, but first a responsibility for the other, that it turns into justice only with the entry of the third party" (*OB*, 190, n. 35). (Here the text refers the reader to Chapter V Section 3, to which we shall return). But let us continue this incremental journey in which the third party is detectable on the margins of the Saying of proximity and substitution. Speaking of humanity, in the chapter on proximity, Levinas wonders whether "the homogeneity of this space [of the approach] would be conceivable without the human signification of justice before all difference, and thus without all the motivations of proximity of which justice is the term" (*OB*, 81). So it is that the "demand for justice" allows itself to be woven into the reverse side of the fabric of proximity (*OB*, 81–83: "The representation of signification is itself born in the signifyingness of proximity insofar as a third party is alongside the neighbor" (*OB*, 83). The text is insistently punctuated by references to the third party and to justice: "It is the proximity of the third party that introduces, with the necessities of justice, measure, thematization, appearing, and justice" (*OB*, 196, n. 22). At this stage, the comparison between humans established by justice appears to unsay the Saying of substitution, which excluded the "possibility of comparison" (*OB*, 127). The contrast is admitted and assumed: speaking of the dissymmetry proper to accusation and the accusative, Levinas notes: "Whatever be the ways that lead to the superstructure of society, in justice the dissymmetry that holds me at odds with regard to the other will find again law, autonomy, equality" (*OB*, 127). But who is the third party? The question is of considerable importance considering what is at stake: "The fact that the other, my neighbor, is also a third party with respect to another, who is also a neighbor, is the birth of thought, consciousness, justice, and philosophy" (*OB*, 128). Here we see outlined the thesis that I will later defend, which links justice, truth, and the possibility of philosophical discourse. But let us develop the idea of the other's other and—why not?—the one who is other than the other, my neighbor. A proximity redoubled by division.

It is in Chapter V, to which footnotes and brief remarks repeatedly refer, that the question of the third party, of justice and of truth is posed the most directly, with full force, I dare say. A first salvo rings out: "What in this signifying, in this one-for-the-other, can and must lead to knowing, to questioning . . . what in this signifying leads to ontology and thus to presence, to manifestation, to the shadowless high noon of truth, to reckoning, thought, settling down, institution—we will no doubt have to show" (*OB*, 137). The terms "third party" and "justice" are not uttered, but the reprise, the repetition, the resaying of knowledge are anticipated as the horizon of the third party and of justice. Here, the text is ahead of the third party. We read that responsibility (which is proximity) "is troubled and becomes a problem with the entry of the third party. The third party is other than the neighbor, but is also another neighbor, and also a neighbor of the Other [capital O], and not simply its fellow" (*OB*, 157). One should read this whole page, where Isaiah 57;19 is quoted: "Peace to all men, both near and far." The prince of this secondary subversion, this subversion of subversion, if one dare say, is enormous: "The third party introduces a contradiction in Saying, whose signification before the other until then went in one direction. . . . Justice is necessary, that is, comparison, coexistence, contemporaneity, assembling, order, thematization, the *visibility* of faces and, thus, intentionality and intellect . . . the intelligibility of a system, and thence also a copresence on an equal footing as before a court of justice" (*OB*, 157). Even more energetically: "The entry of the third party is . . . the comparison of incomparables, thematization of the Same on the basis of the relationship with the Other, on the basis of proximity and the immediacy of Saying . . . " (*OB*, 158). And again: "Justice requires the contemporaneity of representation. It is in this

way that the neighbor becomes visible, and, looked at [*dé-visagé*], presents itself, and that there is also justice for me. Saying is fixed in a said,
is written, becomes a book, law and science" (*OB*, 159).

We have said enough about this to venture a clear hypothesis: the
position of the third party, the place from which justice speaks, is also
the place from which Levinas speaks, inasmuch as *his* Saying is inscribed in a Said which is the book we read. I once caught a furtive admission of this: "The very discourse that we are at this moment elaborating about signification, dia-chrony, and the transcendence of the
approach beyond being, a discourse that means to be philosophy, is a
thematization, a synchronization of terms, a recourse to systematic
language, a constant use of the verb *to be*, bringing back into the bosom
of being all signification allegedly conceived beyond being. But are we
being duped by this subreption?" (*OB*, 155). "The very discourse that
we are at this moment elaborating. . . . " The word "subreption" is
quite strange: it appears again on page 156, upheld by the localization
of the place "in which the present exposition itself claims to stand"
(*OB*, 156–57). Justice is not only the place of the state, it is the place of
truth and of essence, whose "order . . . is in the first rank of Western
philosophy" (*OB*, 156–57). Here, Levinas is unsettled: "Why have we
gone to seek *essence* in its empyrean? Why knowledge? Why is there a
problem? Why philosophy?" (*OB*, 157). Instead of answering from the
place of the question, he takes a quick step back: "We must therefore
follow, in signification or proximity or *Saying*, the latent birth of cognition and essence, of the Said, the latent birth of the *question* in responsibility" (*OB*, 157). If I understand correctly, to call oneself a
philosopher, one cannot be satisfied with the tropes of obsession and
hostage taking, or with the "traumatic violence" professed above (*OB*,
127). One must also *question* responsibility, discern "the latent birth
of the *question* in responsibility." For my part, I am unable to arbitrate
between two readings: on one side, the proposition of a leap from the
near to the far, from the face that does not appear to justice, which
makes faces "visible"; on the other side, the evocation of a "latent
birth," but a "latent birth of knowledge in proximity" (*OB*, 157).
Should one not suspect such a latent birth of "subreption," based on
the preceding discourse?

I shall finish this section on the third party and justice as the site of
philosophical discourse by quoting these particularly explicit lines:

"But does the reason characteristic of justice, the State, thematization, synchronization, the re-presentation of the *logos* and being not succeed in absorbing into its coherence the intelligibility of the proximity in which it flourishes?" (*OB*, 167). Notice the interrogative turn taken here, as also Levinas's subsequent statement that "this is true of the discourse I am elaborating at this very moment" (*OB*, 170).

3—Repetition of ontology?

Once this extremely advanced point has been reached, one wonders whether *Otherwise than Being* contains the beginnings of a post-ethics that would be a way of re-saying the tradition. Does the writing of this book draw on the only benefit offered by the step from dissymmetrical substitution to equalizing justice? I will venture the following outline.

Yes, there is indeed in Levinas's work a quasi-ontology that might be called post-ethical. I detect this ontology in several themes—in the strong sense of the word "theme," "thematic," that is, Said—which, to my mind, exceed the ethics of responsibility. I have chosen four that I will simply list here.

First comes *goodness* and the recourse to the Platonic Good, which, as is well known, is beyond *ousia* (many are the quotes referring to this breakthrough, so to speak, of the responsibility that accuses and wounds).

Next comes *Infinity*, envisioned, it seems beyond the neighbor and the third party, following the exorbitant trajectory of this entire violent tropology. Here as well, the references abound. To the cycle of Infinity belong two connected themes: "the glory of the infinite" and "bearing witness," which I comment on in *Lectures III*.

Then comes *illeity*, spilling over into the third person, which Buber's Thou risks capturing in a too innocent intimacy. I will only mention one text, which curiously brings together illeity and "thirdness" (*OB*, 150). Perhaps other texts that I did not find could clear up these enigmatic lines, as well as those on page 167.

Finally, this list culminates with the *Name* of God inasmuch as it bursts forth in Levinas's own philosophical discourse. This exceptional *Name* signals the revenge of the name over the initial condemnation of denomination, which served as a weapon in the war against ontology. In a sense, this return of the name has a wider significance linked to the question of the *signifyingness* of Saying, as an exception to what

is called the signification of the Said. We saw above how nominalization recovers the verb to the benefit of the substantivized said. But there
is a moment in the process of signifying that requires the name as ex-
ception. This is the very appearing of the face as *individual*. This is
clearly not the Ego, but the ungeneralizable I that I am: "Not Saying
dissimulating itself and protecting itself in the Said" (*OB*, 15), but vul-
nerable, exposing itself to outrage and to wounding (ibid). Subjectivity,
we are reminded, is not a modality of essence, as attested by its Saying
in the Said of the proper name. It is no accident in this context that God
is named for the first time on page 149: Is he not the Name? The Name
that signs signifyingness, without which Saying without the said
would veer toward the ineffable? A Name that does not thematize and
yet signifies. From this Name radiate all other names. And with names
comes the question *who?*—what Levinas dares to call *quis-nity* (*OB*,
25). The other to whom . . . I to whom . . . Not a theme, as are the what
and the how. The question of the name—both God's name and proper
names—covers the whole range of signifyingness beyond signification.
In this range circulate names under the horizon of the Name. A Name
outside of essence or beyond being, "But the Name outside of essence
or beyond essence, the individual prior to Individuality, is named God.
It precedes all divinity, that is, the divine essence to which, like individuals sheltered in their concept, false gods lay claim" (*OB*, 190, n. 38).
With that I leave this Name without theology, which is abandoned to
illusion (*OB*, 94). It is under the aegis of this Name that the "infinite"
may fall into ethics, whereas "totality" falls back into ontology.

Do I dare fire off a final salvo? The text itself authorizes me to do
so. An old theme resurfaces at the end of *Otherwise than Being*, the
theme of the *there is*. One has to wait until the strange final section,
appropriately entitled "Said Otherwise," in order to see reappear the
Gorgon's head of the *there is*, a term expressing the nausea of being
faced with the ever-reborn possibility of non-sense in which the two
adversaries—being and responsibility, ontology and ethics—would
simultaneously cancel each other out: "The claustration of this di-
lemma, of *Essence:* to the anxiety of death is added the horror of fatal-
ity, of the incessant bustling of the *there is*, the horrible eternity at the
bottom of *Essence*" (*OB*, 176). We have asked ourselves throughout
these pages whether all meaning proceeds from *Essence*. But what if
there were no meaning? If ignorance and oblivion were the last word?
Fear of dying or horror of the *there is*, it's all the same . . . (*OB*, 170). To
which there is no response—for want of a guarantee—other than *ex-*

posure, the *passivity of enduring,* in short, the recourse to justice, to the face-to-face of proximity and substitution, to "the crushing burden, the beyond, of alterity" (*OB,* 181). For "Saying [is] always betrayed by the Said" (*OB,* 181).

One more word: with justice can one not hope for the return of memory, beyond the condemnation of the memorable? Otherwise, how could Emmanuel Levinas have written this sober dedication: "To the memory of those who were closest. . ."?

—Translated by Matthew Escobar

PHILIPPE CRIGNON

Figuration:
Emmanuel Levinas and the Image

The problem that concerns us here is figuration. Not the image, and not art, even though, of course, these themes are not unrelated to the arguments that follow. My initial hypothesis is that our current understanding of all these phenomena would benefit from our adopting a new perspective, from our yielding neither to an aesthetic line of inquiry, full of preconceptions about the beautiful, the work, and its meaning, nor to the more recent promotion of the incarnated image, which brilliantly summarizes a certain history but appears incapable of dealing with the new images produced during the last century (cinema, for example) and their anthropological, technical, and political stakes. This is why it seems necessary to ask a simple question: What is it that fundamentally drives man to produce images, to leave traces that are not read but seen and that touch us—to produce not signs, but figures?

Returning to the act of production—to the compulsion to figure— we can expand our field of analysis beyond the narrow sphere of art and include children's drawings, graffiti, and techniques of image production (photography, video, etc.). We can also depart, historically, from the tradition of the Christian image, of the icon and its incarnational model,[1] so that the Lascaux paintings are as much at issue as Boltanski's installations or Fritz Lang's films.

To orient ourselves, let us take as our point of departure a famous image on which Georges Bataille—and not Emmanuel Levinas, who will be the focus here—has extensively commented.[2] It is the image

1. See M.-J. Mondzain's *Image, icône, économie. Les sources byzantines de l'imaginaire contemporain* (Paris: Seuil, 1996), which carefully retraces the constitution and development of this tradition.
2. Georges Bataille, *Lascaux, or The Birth of Art*, trans. Austryn Wainhouse (Lausanne: Skira, 1955), 117, 139–40; *L'érotisme* (Paris: Minuit, 1957), 82–84; *Les larmes d'Éros* (Paris: Pauvert, 1964), 62–65.

YFS 104, *Encounters with Levinas*, ed. Thomas Trezise, © 2004 by Yale University.

known as the "The Man in the Well," which figures among the Lascaux paintings. The rarity of anthropomorphic images in wall paintings is a well-known enigma. For what reasons did the first people prefer to paint beasts rather than their fellow human beings? And why, in the rare cases where human beings did represent themselves, did graceful lines become contorted, arabesques rigid, and forms caricatured?

One can only be astonished by the difficulties encountered in representing human beings, as if they resisted imaging or figuration. Looking at the scene of the well more closely, one notices that the hand that drew it was thwarted by two poles of the human body: the face—reduced to some sort of bird's head, and the sexual organ—unrealistically erect. We will take this figure as a pretext, then, for inquiring about the ties that bind the image to the human body: Why does the image "fail" when it attempts to represent this body? Does this "failure" not teach us something essential about the image—perhaps less about its representational limits than about its real vocation? Conversely, do we not find ourselves confronted with the necessity of rethinking this unfigurable human body, which is at odds with the visible, and of rethinking it on the basis of this very unfigurability, that is, on the basis of this bipolarization— the face and the erotic body—as *exposure* and *exhibition?*

To begin to respond to all these questions, to finally address the problem of figuration, we will study the texts of Levinas, for three main reasons. First, because Levinas tries to found ethics by wresting the Face of man from visibility, by freeing it from the image that it is forever tempted to lapse into. Second, because he recognizes that if our visual perception breaks down before the face of the Other, it is also defeated by its nudity. The ethical and the erotic would stand in sharp contrast to sensible experience and would explain why no representation of the human body is possible. However, the problem for us will then be knowing whether it is really possible to separate the body from the image that lays claim to it. Does not the fact that a vast iconomachy has to be waged—of which the proscription of images is an inevitable consequence—already sufficiently indicate that the image is constantly reborn from this body that wishes to purify itself of it?

There is, then, a third reason to turn to Levinas in order to clarify the question of the image. Levinas is in fact the only philosopher of modernity who did not share in the general enthusiasm for the arts, and in particular, for painting. That he was a fierce and unwavering iconoclast leads us to suspect that he perceived, perhaps better than others, something considerable at stake in the image.

THE NON-PHENOMENALITY OF THE
HUMAN BODY: ETHICS AND EROS

It is well-known that the path Levinas invites us to take consists in beginning with phenomenology in order to turn it around and show its metaphysical condition: ethics. Phenomenology, which describes the constitutive activity of consciousness in each of its acts, shows its limits when faced with the unconstitutable. In other words, it fails when, in the heart of my world, there arrives what I could not draw from myself, an existent [*étant*] whose meaning cannot be attributed to the power of a transcendental subject. This meaning can only be, precisely, that of the incommensurable, of infinite difference, of absolute alterity, of the Other who is not another (second) me. This alterity, strictly speaking, can never be perceived since to see is already to have—if only to have *before one's eyes*—and therefore to possess and to grasp, to dominate and keep. Of course, before becoming knowledge, visual perception is a spectacle in which I revel. But whether it is in enjoyment or in knowledge, the visible is the assimilable, the assimilated. The alterity of the Other cannot therefore stem from any sort of visibility. The Other, as such, does not appear in my world. It does not stand out on any of my horizons, for it is not an object. And yet, unless we return to a spiritual and inaccessible interiority, distinct from a perceived body-object, or to the Cartesian idea of a physical behavior indicating a psychological reality and, thus, to the idea of a sign and an intelligibility of the other as an alter ego modeled on the ego, we must paradoxically concede that alterity arises in the realm of the sensible. The Other, which cannot appear, must nevertheless break in, and thus break in *somewhere*. This *somewhere*, as we know, is the face.

How, then, can the prevalence of ethics over phenomenology be maintained if alterity requires a tangible support, if the face, which is irreducible to a phenomenon, must nevertheless be given in an "*epiphany*"? Levinas would certainly not subscribe to the idea—the very threatening idea—of a "tangible support." And with good reason. That alterity comes about, that it is an event, undergone rather than lived, is an undeniable fact—undeniable because at the very least we know that it is the condition of possibility of all phenomena, as Husserl himself had established.[3] That it occurs implies therefore the localization

_____

3. "The transcendental constitution of other subjects . . . is indispensable to the possibility of an Objective world for me" (Edmund Husserl, *Cartesian Meditations: An In-*

of its epiphany while excluding the phenomenality of its presentation to me. It is with the notion of expression that Levinas manages, in *Totality and Infinity*, to elucidate this paradox. The face is pure expression. Expression is not signification; contrary to the latter, it does not succeed the form it animates, and does not presuppose the existence of an object that, moreover, would refer to another reality. Expression precedes language and the split between signifier and signified. Above all, expression leaves an impression on me. It does so first of all because it is inconceivable and unforeseeable, because none of my horizons makes it possible. Expression is therefore pure meaning and is without context.[4] And the face is not a signifying phenomenon (which is what an animal face would be, signifying fear, hunger, or aggressiveness, for example). This is why Levinas can add: "In this sense one can say that the face is not 'seen.' It is what cannot become a content, which your thought would embrace; it is the uncontainable, it leads you beyond" (*EI*, 86–87). To be sure, "the face expresses itself in the sensible," but it "rends the sensible" (*TI*, 198). It has "its way of incessantly upsurging outside of its plastic image" (*TI*, 262). All of these formulations attempt to mke one think this necessary paradox: that absolute alterity— absolute in the sense that it is not relative to me, that it does not enter into a relation with me[5]—comes to me nevertheless. Or that the beyond-this-world ("the face, which is not of the world" [*TI*, 198]) springs up in a place within my world.

As a place, the face has a form, and as expression it undoes this very form ("The face . . . breaks through the form that nevertheless delimits it" [*TI*, 198]).[6] We already see here what problems representation, if not the reproduction of the face, can pose for the plastic arts. On the one hand, not being a phenomenon, the face is strictly invisible, and thus unfigurable, unless it is reduced to its plastic mask, its purely

---

troduction to Phenomenology, trans. Dorion Cairns [The Hague: Martinus Nijhoff, 1960], 92).

4. "The face signifies by itself" (*TI*, 261).

5. The term "relation" is obviously not the best, but how can we do without it? Levinas will later confess that he prefers the term "approach" ("Interview with François Poirié (1986)," in *Is It Righteous to Be?: Interviews with Emmanuel Levinas*, ed. Jill Robbins [Stanford: Stanford University Press, 2001], 57).

6. There are numerous similar formulations; for example: "The existent breaks through all the envelopings and generalities of Being to spread out in its 'form' the totality of its 'content,' finally abolishing the distinction between form and content" (*TI*, 51). See also *TI*, 65–66, 74–75.

anatomical morphology, that which death substitutes for the face.[7] On the other hand, if the face is not seen, it is at least that which sees: the orientation of the gaze is exactly reversed in the case of artistic representation, where the work—a drawing, painting, sculpture, film, or image of any kind—abandons itself entirely and immoderately to the eye of the spectator. There would thus be a double violence in the figuration of the face: the violence of a human face reduced to the somatic place of its epiphany, and the violence of the desecrating exposure of an enucleated or blind face. In fact, we should not exclude the possibility that the representation of the face, and, in its wake, perhaps all figuration, participates in a certain violence or an impulsive wounding [*griffure*].

Indeed, violence can only be exercised on a target, a surface; but at the same time, violence can only express itself in its infinite powerlessness, its powerlessness to destroy the moral resistance of the face (*TI*, 197, 199). A play of commensurable forces is not yet war, but a natural mechanism, foreign to evil. War and violence only appear when the Other, in its transcendence, defies the very idea of power. This transcendence reveals itself in human features.

Levinas does not call "formlessness" [*l'informe*] the absence of form that the face assumes,[8] but, curiously, "nudity,"[9] a term that supposedly characterizes the state of a body. In reality, the adjective "naked," when attributed to the face, designates not foremost (yet also—and this is another way of formulating the preceding paradox) the state of uncovered skin, but, on the one hand, the absence of protection or defense (the exposure to violence), and on the other, the absence of phenomenality. However, the fact of being without form—nudity—which, as we have seen, guarantees the irreducibility of the face to the world of phenomena, also characterizes the body in its erotic dimension. Form belongs to things, objects of enjoyment or knowledge, what we can possess or see. For "the forms of objects call for the hand and the grasp. By the hand the object is in the end comprehended, touched, taken, borne and *related* to other objects, assumes [*revêt*] a signification, in *relation*

---

7. "The dead face becomes a form, a mortuary mask; it is shown instead of letting see—but precisely thus no longer appears as a face" (*TI*, 262).

8. Formlessness would be a deficiency or privation, whereas not having a form is, for the face as for the flesh, a positive determination: "The face has no form added to it, but does not present itself as the formless, as matter that lacks and calls for form" (*TI*, 140).

9. "The face is not resplendent as a form clothing a content, as an *image*, but as the nudity of the principle" (*TI*, 262).

to other objects" (*TI*, 191).[10] Form occults, offers a surface that covers a depth, a front hiding what lies behind: "Beneath form, things conceal themselves" (*TI*, 192). The face and sexual organs break with this universal morphology by presenting themselves in the mode of nudity: they expose themselves, diversely no doubt—and Levinas does not fail to point out everything that sets them in opposition. Yet the sexual organ, no more than the face, does not hide behind forms: "In the caress . . . the body already denudes itself of its very form, offering itself as erotic nudity" (*TI*, 258).[11] The caress is not prehension, it grasps nothing, and does not expect anything from the thing; it is a contact that holds back, for what it touches—what it approaches [*ce à quoi elle touche*]—is no less scarcely a phenomenon than the face itself. And the paradox that we have noted with respect to the face also applies to the erotic body: naked, without form, the sexual organ that takes us beyond phenomena manifests itself—exhibits itself—in the sensible world that it rends.[12]

We can understand, then, that it is with the same vocabulary and with similar conceptual schemas that Levinas first describes the ethical encounter (with the face) and the erotic encounter (with the sexual organ). Both dismantle the status of the transcendental subject that confronts them, as well as its sovereignty, so true is it that the "I think" always hides a self-satisfied "I can" (predict, grasp, modify, utilize . . .). Each of them introduces the same destabilization, and it is once again a single term that Levinas will employ several pages later to define this destabilization: "My arbitrary freedom reads its shame in the eyes that look at me" (*TI*, 252). This is the effect of the face-to-face. It should be compared with the following formulation: "The shame of profanation

10. It is to be noted that, for Levinas, the verb "revêtir" is not limited to its most common usage [to assume, take on, a given characteristic], but also suggests that form, signification—*Sinngebung*—would clothe phenomena. Clothing or uniform insures integration within the same. Thus, it is opposed to the nudity of the face and the sensual flesh. These, because they express an infinite alterity, do not assume [or "put on"] any signification.

11. On the preceding page we read: "The caress consists in seizing upon nothing, in soliciting what carelessly escapes its form toward a future . . ." (*TI*, 257).

12. The caress, as a mode of access to the erotic body, is "a relation yet, in one aspect, sensible" (*TI*, 258). "The caress, like contact, is sensibility. But the caress transcends the sensible" (*TI*, 257). The sensual is no more sensible than the face is visible. To be sure, there is always, "in one aspect," as Levinas would say, a vision of the face (this expression recurs several times in *Totality and Infinity*), but it is "the vision of the very openness of being, it cuts across the vision of forms and can be stated neither in terms of contemplation nor in terms of practice" (*TI*, 193).

lowers the eyes that should have scrutinized the uncovered" (*TI*, 260). This is the effect of exhibited flesh. Shame, a common effect of shared nudity, points to the singular relationship that unites the human face and the sexual organ of the other. That the one and the other are formally opposed, that the shame they incite does not have the same meaning on both sides, should not make us forget what links them, what even renders them indissociable, for it is precisely in this sharing alone that their asymmetry can be understood.

If both the face and the sexual organ are characterized as non-phenomena, if all form is taken away from them, and if therefore any possibility of seeing or grasping them is ruled out,[13] we can understand why the figuration of the human being runs up against these two poles, how it can only be problematic. A line cannot possibly follow what eludes the gaze. No technique, be it manual or not, can retranscribe or record the invisible. To understand the ethical and the erotic is to consent to the collapse of the aesthetic. The face and the sexual organ, as the man of Lascaux seems to suggest, are unfigurable. Not that the rest of the human anatomy remains entirely untroubled. On the contrary, as Levinas makes clear, "the whole body—a hand or a curve of the shoulder—can express like the face" (*TI*, 262). It would be absurd if the face were the only part of the body that must not be struck! Similarly, as we shall see, the erotic charge can contaminate other parts of the body (to say nothing of fetishism, as, for example, in the disturbed perception that Flaubert had of the female foot), the whole body and the face itself.

We would thus be led to extend the impossibility of being figured to the human body as a whole. Anthropomorphism would be excluded from the plastic arts, or more precisely, would be beyond their reach. However—and even if certain religions turn this factual impossibility into a proscription—all of art history contradicts such a conclusion, beginning with two of the most important pictorial traditions that our culture has known, namely, the tradition of the portrait,[14] on the one hand, and the tradition of the nude,[15] on the other.

Thus, it is not sufficient to establish the non-phenomenality of the face and the sexual organ, their invisibility in a non-metaphorical

13. "Voluptuousness profanes; it does not see" (*TL*, 260).
14. See, for example, Tzvetan Todorov, *Éloge de l'individu. Essai sur la peinture flamande de la Renaissance* (Paris: A. Biro, 2000).
15. See, for example, Kenneth Clark, *The Nude: A Study in Ideal Form* (New York: Pantheon, 1956).

sense, nor the apparently insurmountable pitfalls that this creates for their representation. We must still understand why they are figured nonetheless. Simply put, this is because the obstacles *to* figuration reveal what figuration *is,* because one suspects figuration to be compulsively anthropomorphic—face and sexual organ, ethical and erotic—before being an aesthetic operation. Curiously, Levinas comes down here on the side of someone like Bataille, from whom, however, almost everything separates him. Nevertheless, Bataille, in his own way, linked sacred trembling and erotic spasms to figuration.[16] To be sure, their points of departure are diametrically opposed: Bataille, in fact, begins with the image (the Lascaux paintings or Manet) and draws out the sacred stakes of the game; and he can do this because he situates himself from the outset within the religious and ritual spheres he is investigating. Levinas, for his part, undertakes to describe what is before all possible images and representations at the very moment he admits that the erotic body contains the possibility of figuration.

How can the fact of figuration be understood, once the non-phenomenality of the face and sexual organ is admitted? What is required here, as we can now see, is that the work of art not be a representation or an image as Levinas understands them. In order to elucidate the close ties that unite art, ethics, and the erotic, however, we will once again follow Levinas. We will see that it is in the interference of sexuality with the face-to-face that beauty is produced, a beauty that art will, according to him, continually present, put into form, render visible. Considering art, then, as a poetry that charms, bewitches, and evacuates responsibility [*déresponsabilise*], Levinas will condemn it without reservation. It is by putting the two texts to work—beginning with *Totality and Infinity*[17]—that we will try to see how such a judgment could have been informed and what the meaning of such an exclusion is. To be sure, the question of art is not essential for Levinas: no analysis of his deals with it after 1948, but several times, and often in critical places, the work of art (essentially plastic, as we shall see) intervenes in order to underscore a contrast or conclude a remark. Let us state in

16. For example, in *L'érotisme,* Bataille speaks of the Lascaux painting and links it to profanation: "The play of figuration was a response to the play of transgression" (83).

17. We will later address the essential modifications contributed by *Otherwise than Being* and the texts surrounding it. The work of art is partly rehabilitated there, from the moment that Levinas acknowledges its expressivity, similar in kind to that of cultural objects and gestures. But the image remains that which makes us forget the other. Let us recall, though, that Levinas devoted two texts to the painters Atlan and Sosno.

advance that these texts offer two means of access to the question of art. The first considers the work of art as a particular case of the work [*l'oeuvre*] in general. As such, the work of art assumes a signification but no longer expresses anything; it is an image in the sense of representation. The second follows the trace of beauty—from its appearance in the epiphany of the female face to the grace of the work of art—which is immediately declared superficial since it is the beauty of a surface, of an image. The question of the work, then, and the question of the beautiful, even when combined, do not suffice to question the work of art *in its essence.* These two paths reveal, no doubt, not so much the failure of a certain method as the irreducibility of the work of art to an essence, the impossibility of gaining access to art by metaphysical means, and the fact that any metaphysics finds itself in the end obliged to denounce it.

DOUBLE NUDITY

The absence of form, nudity, can be understood in two ways.[18] In the case of the face, it is destitution, exposure, and distress, but also revelation, full presence, and laying bare, irreducible to the phenomenal world that I constitute. The face-to-face introduces the amorphous, the existent [*étant*] par excellence, in other words, that which is not the object of a *Sinngebung*, which is not integrated into the world of significations because it is the absolute expression of a presence. As meaning per se, however, the face is also the origin of meaning, of language, and thus of phenomena and the world. Invisible, it is the origin of visibility. Devoid of form, it makes forms possible. Nevertheless, the epiphany of the face that occurs in the present of the face-to-face seems condemned not to survive itself: "I will not always be here," says the face in its extreme fragility. Death or history threatens discourse and its truth. In the final analysis, the necessity of finding an alterity that averts its neutralization by history and the pitfall of death is what impels Levinas to seek a "beyond the face," which he finds in what he names Eros.

The erotic body is also without form, but in a way completely different from that of the face. What is exposure for the one is exhibition

18. If not in three ways, but the third—the nudity of things, their absence of decorum—is metaphorical ("Things are naked, by metaphor, only when they are unadorned" [*TI*, 74]), which, again, is enough to say that the nudity of the face and the nudity of the sexual organ are (also) literal.

for the other. For the one, nudity expresses frankness and vulnerability; for the other, it is shamelessness, indecency, and ambiguity. This is because, according to Levinas, the nudity of the sexual organ is "profanation," a term that places us right away in the domain of the sacred: profanation uncovers what should have remained hidden, what *therefore* remains hidden even when uncovered. The sexual organ is, at once, too much and too little for the eye. In its exhibition, it imposes on the gaze an excess of materiality that explodes all form, an "ultramateriality" that is "exorbitant," to use Levinas's term. Nudity becomes crudity, irreducible to the acclimation under which every phenomenon appears. It is thus not a phenomenon, and even less an accident (to be undressed), but the way of being of the sexual organ. Conceptual rigor forces us here to say that the erotic approach brings us into relation, not with a phenomenon, but with an epiphany[19]—another word that Eros shares with its double, the face. There remains nevertheless a difference, in that while the face expresses itself, the sexual organ profanes. The face-to-face is not the body-to-body. In its sacrilegious dimension, the body that offers itself naked reveals that it hides or continues to hide what it shows, and for this reason expresses nothing.

However, love and desire are directed at the other. They address themselves to a person: the erotic body is first a body that has a face. The profanation of the exhibited sexual organ points toward the expression of the face and is possible only because of it: "Elements and things remain outside of respect and disrespect. It is necessary that the face be perceived for nudity to acquire the non-signifyingness of the lustful" (*TI*, 262). Here Levinas establishes the ethical implication in the erotic. That this implication is reciprocal is something Levinas would never admit, but it is also perhaps here that metaphysics, in its need for a first principle and a simple origin, finds its limits.

The sexual organ thus does not efface the face: it would disappear along with it. But it is its parasite; it introduces confusion, a double meaning, equivocation, and suspends discourse, provoking an ambiguous silence. Voluptuousness is equivocal in that it is at once enjoyment or consumption and their exact opposite: self-dispossession (as in Bataille's notion of the orgasm [*la "petite mort"*—literally "little

---

19. "An epiphany of the Beloved, the feminine is not added to an object and a Thou antecedently given or encountered in the neuter, the only gender known to formal logic. The epiphany of the Beloved is but one with her *regime* of tenderness" (*TI*, 256). It is elsewhere stated, for example, that "equivocation constitutes the epiphany of the feminine" (*TI*, 264). This expression is used repeatedly in *Totality and Infinity*.

death"], although it is true that Levinas refuses the idea of ecstasy).[20] We have seen that a caress is not a seizure, but a hand that seeks without ever finding. This is not because of a defect—unless we stubbornly insist on a schema where taking possession remains the norm, in which case it does in fact correspond to a failure—but because a caress is not the first movement of grasping. It is rather a radically different way of approaching the other, the particular self-sufficient way of relating to the other's flesh. From this proposition, Levinas concludes that Eros does not put me in relation with anything that is a presence, an existent, but, on the contrary, with something that always eludes me in a "later," that is always to come.[21] In the end, it is not the face (the relationship of Me to You) that institutes the most radical alterity, but sexuality (where the Me abandons itself in its own fecundity):[22] "In sexuality the subject enters into relation with what is absolutely other . . . with what remains other in the relation and is never converted into 'mine' " (*TI*, 276).

THE IMAGE AS ORNAMENT OF THE BODY

We have only apparently strayed from the question of figuration. In fact, if we recall what the man of Lascaux orients us toward—the figuration of two unrepresentables, the face and the sexual organ, or to put it differently, anthropomorphic figuration, figuration *as* anthropomorphism—we come back to the amorphous double epiphany that Levinas describes, or rather to the coincidence of these epiphanies as the advent of figuration. If by its ontological structure (the face is an existent—the existent par excellence—whereas the carnal is no longer one at all)[23] and its particular temporality (the face-to-face is played out in the present whereas the erotic relation opens an absolutely new fu-

20. See *TO*, 41.
21. It is not the verb "to be" that is inadequate, when used in reference to the flesh of the other, but the *present* participle of the existent [*l'étant*]. The sexual organ does the same "work" [*"métier"*] of being as the face—to use an expressive term of which Levinas is fond—but does not partake of the same temporality. Following the example of the present and past participle, we would need to invent a *future* participle to designate the ontological status of the erotic body: a *"serant."*
22. Another problem: Is fecundity the only perspective of an authentic Eros? The question is whether absolute alterity is maintained without the inspiration of paternity. One can argue against Levinas that a non-procreative sexuality does not end up in possession (whose very "possessiveness" would arguably indicate a powerlessness), and that it is, in its way, an indefinitely reiterated defection and a temporization.
23. "In the face, the existent par excellence presents itself " (*TI*, 262). On the contrary, "in the carnal given to tenderness, the body quits the status of an existent" (*TI*, 258).

ture),[24] the transcendence of the Other is not that of Eros, the erotic body nevertheless refers to the face. The latter is thus not impermeable to sensuality. No doubt we can even add that the greatest sensuality springs up where it should manifest itself the least, in its greatest pro-fanatory force, namely, in the face. Nothing is more erotic than a face become lascivious, for this is the greatest transgression. The eroticized, or "feminine" face,[25] as Levinas says, is at once the beginning and the culmination of eroticism. In it, "the purity of expression is already trou-bled by the equivocation of the voluptuous" (TI, 260). Let us finally quote the passage that concerns us here:

> This presence of non-signifyingness in the signifyingness of the face, or this reference of non-signifyingness to signifyingness—where the chastity and decency of the face abides at the limit of the obscene yet repelled but already close at hand and promising—is the primordial event of feminine beauty, of that eminent sense that beauty assumes in the feminine, but which the artist will have to convert into "weightless grace" by carving in the cold matter of color or stone, where beauty will become calm presence, sovereignty in flight, existence unfounded for without foundations [sans fondements car sans fondations]. [TI, 263]

The beautiful is thus the equivocation of a decency troubled by voluptuousness, the equivocation of nudity itself, secretive and desti-tute all at once. The first moment of beauty does not reside after all in works of art—and even less in nature—but in the feminine, that is, in Eros. And even though it is not a phenomenon, it comes to be in the immediate proximity of the face. The work of art is only beautiful with reference to this original beauty. We see, then, that the itinerary con-ceived by Levinas to lead to the question of figuration—or rather, one of the two itineraries leading there—includes three stages: the face in its uprightness, the face besieged by equivocation, and the work of art.

24. "The encounter with the Other as feminine is required in order that the future of the child come to pass from beyond the possible, beyond projects. . . . The relation with the child—that is, the relation with the other that is not a power, but fecundity—estab-lishes relationship with the absolute future, or infinite time" (TI, 267–68).

25. The identification of the lascivious and the feminine—which is neither a simple residual bias nor an inessential characterization for the very meaning of alterity—can-not be taken up here at any length. To see in it a metaphor does not resolve the situation, since the reasons for the metaphor would still have to be specified. And it is not certain that a correction like the one put forward by Levinas twenty years later makes the prob-lem any easier ("Perhaps, on the other hand, all these allusions to the ontological differ-ences between the masculine and the feminine would appear less archaic if, instead of dividing humanity into two principles . . . they signified that the participation in the mas-culine and in the feminine were the attribute of every human being" [EI, 68]).

This development is nothing like a straight line, a route that could be traced out on a single surface. From one station to another, the *level* [*plan*] changes—that is, at once the level and the visual features. And the operation that enables movement from one state to another is what Levinas calls conversion, or, more precisely still, *inversion*. Thus, after describing "this inversion of the face in femininity" (*TI*, 262),[26] he declares that "the beautiful of art *inverts* the beauty of the feminine face" (*TI*, 263). The work of art thus has a genealogy, it is the face doubly inverted (which is not a return to its initial position).

Put forth thus, the concept of inversion requires some clarification. It does not mean a contrary (contraries are constituted within a common genus, but no generic or preliminary concept can contain the epiphany of the face), but already a substitution, a supplanting in which a reference to the original epiphany is perpetuated. If sensuality disfigures the face, this disfiguration still "refers to the face" (*TI*, 262). Moreover, inversion implies an order and a priority. It is an irreversible movement: first there is the face, and then its complication in the feminine, the reverse not being possible. What substitution occurs, then, in the artistic process? And at the heart of this new "disfiguration," of this second—and as if squared—"disfiguration" (which is strictly speaking equivalent to figuration), what reference to the feminine face, to the double, troubled epiphany of the sexual Other is maintained?

For Levinas, art substitutes an image for the feminine that lives, exposes itself, and exhibits itself all at once. In a clear, distinct manner, he only conceives of artistic activity as a plastic immobilization, a molding of what, by essence, could not and should not be fixed. The carnal that escapes toward an absolute future, in the obscurity and mystery that the caress of the lover touches without ever grasping, is absorbed here in a simple thing, that is, in a simple form. The skin that troubles is inverted into a surface. And the surface, itself, no more exposes than it exhibits; on the contrary, it masks. Behind its forms the work of art hides an inert matter, marble or colors: "[The beautiful of art] substitutes an image for the troubling depth of the future, of the 'less than nothing' . . . announced and concealed by feminine beauty. It

26. Inversion, reverse, reversal, contrariety [*inversion, envers, retournement, rebours*] are all equivalent terms describing these essential alterations. "As the reverse of the expression of what has lost expression, [the non-signifyingness of the lascivious] thereby refers to the face" (*TI*, 264); "The hidden . . . is beyond the personal and like its reverse" (*TI*, 264). Correlatively, from the face-to-face to the body-to-body, subjectivity is subjected to a "reversal" (*TI*, 270).

presents a beautiful form reduced to itself in flight, deprived of its depth" (*TI*, 263).[27] Art is a fall into the world of forms, thus a degradation, a paganism, an idolatry. For the work of art gives itself to be seen but remains, itself, blind or enucleated. The work does not see us, does not *look at* us[28]—and thus does not reveal anything. This return to *morphē* is a return to visibility. A painting, a statue can be seen as authentic phenomena. They can be circumvented, for the image does not harbor any infinity: as finitude and an object of enjoyment, the work of art allows for the reconstitution of an ego without any facing alterity.

Strictly speaking, the fact that the image is a phenomenon isolates it from the face from which it derives. But is the image not also *in the likeness* of that of which it is an image? Here the problem of mimesis is raised in an original manner. For it is no longer a question of conceiving of it as the representation of an object, a theme, or a model. It is thus the meaning of the image itself that requires a new understanding. The "resemblance" of the image is nothing more than its quasi-umbilical link with the animated face, and this is what needs to be explained. The inversion of feminine beauty in the work of art retains its reference to this original beauty. Granted, all art is plastic, but all art is the figuration of femininity, that is, portrait and nude, anthropomorphism (which we define once and for all as the *figuration of the double epiphany of the face and the sexual organ*). What does it mean to be a resemblance here, when we no longer understand it as a "realist" representation, a reproduction or copy? In Levinas's article entitled "Reality and Its Shadow," this resemblance is distinguished from the sign, which, for its part, is transparent. Resemblance has a certain opacity: we look at the image, we do not look through the image. It is neither an existent (it is not that of which it is an image) nor a pure nothingness; it is the double of reality, its shadow, its obscuring. Figuration would thus be only a putting into form,[29] an imaging, an inscription in the sensible: a surface that is not even skin but sensitized film, a nega-

---

27. In an earlier text, dating from 1948, and which is like the first investigation of art by ethics, Levinas already describes the artistic process in terms of substitution: "The most elementary procedure of art consists in substituting for the object its image" ("Reality and its Shadow," *CPP*, 3).

28. Levinas speaks of "the gods immobilized in the between-time of art, left for all eternity on the edge of the interval, at the threshold of a future that never occurs, statues looking at one another with empty eyes, idols that, unlike Gyges, are exposed and do not see" (*TI*, 221–22).

29. "Beauty becomes a form covering over indifferent matter, and not harboring mystery" (*TI*, 263).

tive of the real, a photo-*graphy*. And so also a snapshot [*instantané*]. To the living presence of the face, to the absolute future to which the female body opens, one must oppose the immobility of the work of art, its suspension in the "meanwhile."

If we study its temporal aspect, the inversion of feminine beauty through which the work of art is engendered reveals once again the two moments of substitution and internal reference. Immobile image of mobile time, the work of art does not exist under the aspect of eternity, but in suspense, in the interval. The temporality of the work of art is bridled: not a living flux but the repetition of an instant always identical to itself. The Mona Lisa will never finish her smile. But Levinas adds: hence a rhythm.[30] That suspense is also a rhythm (that is, a tempo, a temporalization) should not be surprising. Rhythm is the image of life; it is neither life nor time but their imitation, their caricature.[31] Immobility cannot dominate the temporal mode of the work of art, for it would render it ineffective. The work integrates, therefore, a form of temporal flow that is not life (neither a presence, nor a future authentically to come, irreducible to the present and its possibilities or projects, unanticipatable), but something that nonetheless aspires to life. A vivacity, an aping of time, or what Levinas calls "caricature."

This "caricature" nevertheless fascinates, captivates, and charms its spectator. Through rhythm, through the repetition of the same, the work of art makes us leave the reasonable world of the face-to-face and regress to a state of elementary hedonism. Seized and as if bewitched (witches, for Levinas, are accountable for a bad alchemy in which the

---

30. "Every work of art is painting and statuary, immobilized in the instant or in its periodic return. Poetry substitutes a rhythm for feminine life" (*TI*, 263). "The hold that an image has over us" is, writes Levinas already in 1948, "a function of rhythm" (*CPP*, 5).

31. "The artwork does not succeed, is bad, when it does not have that aspiration for life which moved Pygmalion. But it is only an aspiration. The artist has given the statue a lifeless life, a derisory life that is not master of itself, a caricature of life. . . . *Every image is already a caricature*" (*CPP*, 9). This is not Levinas's last word on art but, quite the contrary, his first. The partial rehabilitation to which he will agree after *Totality and Infinity*—culture's taking on a signal ontological function (assembling of being, celebration of being, whose comprehension it renders possible) and a new meaning ("*Signification and Sense*" [translated as "*Meaning and Sense*," *CPP*, 75–107] makes of the cultural work an expression, something that was until then the prerogative of the face)—does not put into question its secondary, inferior position precisely because, if culture governs ontology, it remains indifferent to ethics, and thus to transcendence. The theses of the 1948 article, although belonging to the first period, are posterior to the lectures published in *Time and the Other* and are connected to the unchanged principles of Levinasian ethics. *Totality and Infinity* and *Otherwise than Being* assume and refer to these theses. See *TI*, 221–22 and *OB*, 199, n. 21.

complicity of eroticism and the work of art takes shape), the ego finds a poetic rhythm imposed on it,[32] relinquishing its mastery but also its responsibility. Art is foreign to discourse, retaining only its material, words, to play with. It is guilty of a rhetoric (verbal, plastic, or sonorous) that subverts language and digests every alterity.

We are surprised to see that it is not "woman," sexuality, the exorbitant exhibition of the other's sexual organ—of the other sex—that fascinate and subjugate, according to Levinas, but paradoxically, the work of art, which, let us recall, is its visible reverse: a painting or film, for example. We should here distinguish charm from seduction, a term that Levinas never uses but that appears to correspond to the power proper to the feminine. The image constrains me permanently when Eros—rather than imprisoning me or coaxing me, that is, rather than confining me in the instant—exiles me, separates me from myself, and invites me to the adventure of a future and an absolute time (fecundity, paternity). It leads me there, which means it seduces me.[33]

THE TWO PRINCIPLES OF THE ICONOCLASM OF *TOTALITY AND INFINITY*

That the inversion of the sensual into the work of art is interpreted as image and resemblance, as a return to forms and visibility, makes the condemnation of art inevitable. But such an interpretation is only possible if we accept two principles that, themselves, lead us back to a common postulate.

At the moment when Levinas advances, in an original way, the idea that artistic beauty is inherited from the beauty of the feminine, he makes it into the attribute of a substance, the adjective of a substantive, the quality of a product. The beautiful is inherited from the feminine but is inscribed in a work, and thus in a form, a visible object. And it is its meaning as work that ultimately ruins, at a first stage, the work of art. It is like a particular case of the genus *opus.* Now, as Levinas insists fairly strongly, the work is a loss, it can no longer help itself, it is

---

32. "To poetic activity—where influences arise unbeknown to us out of this nonetheless conscious activity, to envelop it and beguile it as a rhythm . . . where in a dionysiac mode the artist (according to Nietzsche's expression) becomes a work of art—is opposed the language that at each instant dispels the charm of rhythm and prevents initiative from becoming a role. Discourse is rupture and commencement, a breaking of the rhythm that enraptures and transports the interlocutors—prose" (*TI*, 203).

33. If Eros ravishes (rapture or ravishing is not capture or captivity), it does so "beyond every project" (*TI*, 264).

no longer supported by living speech. Whether a dead letter or a still life [*Lettre morte, nature morte*], the product—be it artistic or not—estranges from itself everything that guaranteed alterity. The work of art is a work to which is simply added a new aesthetic quality, beauty;[34] and the latter does not at all put into question its meaning as work, which is foremost. Levinas reveals himself here to be a strict aesthetician. The work of art is a beautiful work. And, like everything that man makes, no expression, no expressivity radiates in its breast. The face has disappeared: "The work does not defend itself against the Other's *Sinngebung*, and exposes the will that produced it to contestation and unrecognition; it lends itself to the designs of a foreign will and allows itself to be appropriated" (*TI*, 227). The absence of the author in the result of his work marks his refusal to express himself, and thus to address himself to the spectator,[35] and his retreat behind forms. The ethical relation is only produced between interlocutors, in the vis-à-vis, and vanishes in aesthetic contemplation.

The second principle on which is based the process of inversion as it is described by Levinas suggests that inversion institutes an ontological order and priority. First comes the face, then its reverse, the feminine. First the feminine then its reverse, art. First language then its reverse, laughter (the heavy silence of equivocations).[36] By contrast, alterity, for example, is not derived from identity and is thus not its reverse.[37] The carnal needs the face to subsist and refers to it, but the in-

34. Beauty becomes decoration and clothing, ornament—which is why nature can borrow this beauty. To bring the question of art back to that of beauty, as Levinas does in this context, is to deny oneself any means of access to the problem of figuration. This partiality is confirmed, for example, in the following passage: "The aesthetic orientation man gives to the whole of his world represents a return to enjoyment and the elemental on a higher plane. The world of things calls for art, in which intellectual accession to being changes into enjoyment, in which the Infinity of the idea is idolized in the finite, but sufficient, image. All art is plastic. Tools and implements, which themselves presuppose enjoyment, offer themselves to enjoyment in their turn. They are playthings [*jouets*]: the fine cigarette lighter, the fine car. They are adorned by decorative arts; they are immersed in the beautiful, where every going beyond enjoyment reverts to enjoyment" (*TI*, 140). The impasse described here by Levinas is not that of art but of aesthetics.

35. "Through works alone the I does not come outside; it withdraws from it or congeals within it as though it did not appeal to the Other and did not respond to it, but in its activity sought comfort, privacy, and sleep" (*TI*, 176).

36. "Thus silence is not a simple absence of speech; speech lies in the depths of silence like a laughter perfidiously held back. Silence is the reverse of language" (*TI*, 91).

37. "The other sex is an alterity borne by a being as an essence and not as the reverse of its identity" (*TI*, 121). It is indeed Eros that answers the question: "Does a situation exist where the other would not have alterity only as the reverse side of its identity, would

verse implication would not be true. Similarly, artistic activity pre-supposes that we have already encountered erotic desire, but the latter is primary and self-sufficient. Refusing mutual implication means that a world without erotics and a world without art are possible, that the face can present itself in its uprightness without being threatened by obscenity, and that, at bottom, a pure expression, an origin of meaning, exist in it.

Now, it is not clear that this is the case. When Levinas, on several occasions, grounds alterity not in the epiphany of the face but in the epiphany of the feminine,[38] does he not express their co-originarity? The *saltus* that leads us back before ontology and phenomenology, be-fore being and phenomena, opens not only on the face-to-face, but on a face that shares the same skin as the sexual organ, a face that is itself skin. There is nothing prior to the erotic relation, not even a face. Or rather, the face only shines in proximity to an experience of desire. It then shines as primordial even though it was never able to manifest it-self as pure and free of all equivocation. A literal meaning is a chimera, or rather, it is the anteriority that never came to be, the immemorial before, of *figurative* meaning.[39] This being the case, inversion con-serves its meaning but henceforth goes hand in hand with a co-origi-narity of the epiphanies in question. We must therefore recognize that the inversion that leads to the beautiful work, the work of art, demands an equally reciprocal necessity. Art, then, no longer has the contin-gency to which *Totality and Infinity* had confined it; it is as originary as the face or Eros, as the encounter with the Other, that it figures. There is no world without the adventure of art, without anthropomor-phism, any more than there is a world without the Other.

Levinas does not follow this path that binds figuration to the Other. Yet, *Totality and Infinity* leaves unresolved difficulties to which the image is not unrelated. Thus, in this work our relation to the other is conceived as a relation to the face, a pure existent, a substance of Καθ'αυτο. But can we use the category of relation without, at the same

---

not comply only with the Platonic law of participation where every term contains a same-ness and through this sameness contains the other?" (*TO*, 85).

38. The erotic relation founds transcendence (*TI*, 276). The feminine is "the origin of the very concept of alterity" (*EI*, 66, where Levinas refers to the theses of *Time and the Other*).

39. This is, of course, the teaching of Jacques Derrida, *Of Grammatology*, trans. Gay-atri Chakravorty Spivak (Baltimore: The Johns Hopkins University Press, 1976), and *Speech and Phenomena*, trans. David Allison (Evanston: Northwestern University Press, 1973).

time, situating ourselves in rationality, the logos, and representation in consciousness? If the face of the Other can be free of all disturbance, without equivocation, without a body, how could it touch me? But, conversely, if it can touch me, if the face is body, if it weds the skin that calls forth the caress, is it not already a tangible production, already figuration? *Otherwise than Being or Beyond Essence,* and notably its central chapter, "Sensibility and Proximity," attempts to go back beyond the hesitations of *Totality and Infinity* and to think the approach of the Other no longer in a formal manner, as a relation, but in a material and tangible manner. And yet the image always returns, as a drawing or trace, to threaten the purity or holiness of the Other. This is why, each time Levinas speaks of the face, he does so to oppose it to the image. Iconoclasm is now replaced by a great iconomachy.

THE PROHIBITION AGAINST IMAGES: THE IMAGE AND ITS BODY

In *Totality and Infinity,* Levinas acknowledges that the beauty of the work of art is inherited from the beauty of the feminine, and therefore that figuration prolongs the epiphany of the Other's body by inverting it. One might be tempted—and many, from Hegel through Benjamin to Georges Didi-Huberman, have taken the trouble—to say of the figural what Levinas has said of the face: that a painting is more than a visible phenomenon, that it opens onto an invisible sphere, that it looks at me at least as much as I see it, which, despite the divergent formulations that express this—icon, "sensuous presentation of the Idea," incarnated image, "aura"—amounts to a common determination in which a near binds itself to a far and an invisibility is enacted within the visible. Why does Levinas not follow this path? Why does the image remain tied to the model of representation, in the domain of art as well? Why, finally, does he remain an iconoclast? To evoke here the Jewish tradition of proscribing images is not inappropriate to the extent that Levinas himself refers to it in an article from 1981, "The Prohibition against Representation and the 'Rights of Man.'" To be sure, one should not be content with drawing a parallel between an iconoclastic position and a religious affinity. It is rather a question of analyzing what, at the heart of Jewish thought as Levinas elaborates it, authorizes the judgment [*procès*] of images.

The article begins with an explicit reference to the "Jewish tradition" and specifies right from the start the limits of the prohibition against images as understood by this tradition. This prohibition does not concern the illustrations or descriptions of which scientific thinking must make use in order to progress: "All representation is authorized when it is a question of scientific research" (*AT*, 121–22). Consequently, the forbidden images are those that have an end only in themselves, those that are produced not to illustrate or make known but to be seen [*se donner à voir*]. This clarification that Levinas introduces at the outset encourages us, then, to understand proscription as the prohibition *of figuration* (the production of ostensible figures: works of art, ornaments, icons, figurines, etc.). However, it is still in the name of a representation-image, an informative image, that Levinas condemns art.[40] The problem that Levinas faces here is the following: once you admit the relationship between the other's body and figuration (through beauty), and the resemblance between all images and the face,[41] the Other seems to have ties with the visible that are too close and threatens to recede into the sphere of immanence. This is why, on the one hand, Levinas continues to denounce the work of art—but always in a problematic way—and, on the other hand, tries to shield ever more the face and body of the other from the risk of visibility. It is this tension that we need to examine. It reveals two things: the impossibility of separating the image from the body (and the body from the image), and the necessity of not assimilating them, of not incorporating them. The image is always, for Levinas, an image of the face ("the inanimate resembling the face" [*AT*, 123]), but it is also that from which the face must be saved. Levinas, in this sense, is not iconoclastic but iconomachic; it is for him less a matter of having a position than of thinking a tension, a tension that is none other than the power of images to touch us.

THE ATTEMPT TO SHIELD THE BODY
FROM THE IMAGE

Totality and Infinity finally abandons the face to its struggle with its own phenomenality. Henceforth, Levinas will seek to shield the Other

40. "In the 'prohibition against representation' I am only questioning the exclusive privilege that Western culture has conferred on consciousness [*conscience*] and science [*science*]" (*AT*, 125).
41. Thus: "Beneath the plasticity of the face [*figure*] that *appears*, the face [*visage*] is already missed. It is frozen in art itself, despite the artist's possible attempt to disfigure the 'something' that starts again, figurative, in presence" (*AT*, 126).

from the image, to break this robust, persistent link that ties the body to the image. We will analyze this development in four stages:

1. The face conceived as a pure existent, as a substance Καθ'αυτο, and finally as a supreme existent, does not hide its resemblance to God himself. But the very term "resemblance" implies that the face somehow belongs, as much as God (the face of God), to visibility, to the world and its system of reciprocal relations. Against this risk—which Derrida has pointed out[42]—Levinas intends to describe the face as a *trace.* After questioning himself ("Have we been faithful enough to the prohibition against seeking the beyond, as a world behind our world?" [*CPP,* 103]), he reveals the necessity of dissociating the face from any idea of the presentation of Infinity: "The signifyingness of the trace puts us into a 'lateral' relation that cannot be converted into rectitude (something inconceivable in the order of disclosure and being)" (*CPP,* 103). Thus, the face is no longer revelation, as in *Totality and Infinity.* Hence the first shielding from the image: "The God who has passed is not the model of which the face would be the image. To be in the image of God does not mean to be the icon of God, but to find oneself in his trace" (*CPP,* 106).

2. The ethical relation seemed to be produced in the present of a face-to-face. But the present of this "encounter" would presuppose a synchronization of Me and the Other, the existence of a time that would envelop us both and in which the face of the other would *present* itself. The image is presentation (or its modalities: representation, presentification) and is given in the present: "The common hour marked by the clock is the hour in which the neighbor reveals himself and delivers himself in his image, but it is precisely in his image that he is no longer near" (*OB,* 89). The trace is not the present sign of an absence, it refers to an absence that cannot be presented, that cannot therefore be recollected: it leads us toward a past that was never present, toward an immemoriality. The relation to the other is diachronic. This is the second shielding from the image.

3. All the while conceding the possibility of Eros as a perturbation of the face-to-face, Levinas maintained, in *Totality and Infinity,* the irreducible anteriority of the face and the possibility that an ethical relation could be free of any alteration. Eros was indeed "beyond the

42. In "Violence and Metaphysics," in *Writing and Difference,* trans. Alan Bass (Chicago: University of Chicago Press, 1978), Derrida glosses Levinas's sentence: "The Other resembles God."

face." Thus, if the Other was to break into the heart of the world, it could only be by giving itself over to a perception and not a sensation. It took place as something visible (even if undoing its visibility) and not as something tactile. A simple negation of the visible, the face was still available to the gaze. *Otherwise than Being* thinks epiphany as an excess rather than a negation: "It is the superlative, more than the negation of category, that interrupts the system" (*OB*, 187, n. 5). For this, we need an immediacy of the relation of Me to the Other that only the flesh provides. In this book, the face and the sexual organ are intimately imbricated and bound together. If ethics maintains its primacy, it has nevertheless become impossible outside of the carnal relationship: "The-one-for-the-other, exposure of self to another, immediacy in the caress and in the contact of saying—the immediacy of a skin and a face, a skin that is always the modification of a face, of a face that is weighed down with a skin" (*OB*, 85).[43] The implication has become reciprocal, and this change is crucial. Levinas will seek new concepts with which to characterize it. Thus, while Eros remains what it already was—an alteration of the epiphany of the face—the face is now conceived as always already "weighed down" by skin: this term, through its dynamic connotation, encourages us to think henceforth about the organic coexistence of the face and Eros (further reinforced by the promotion of the term "skin": how could a face be without skin?) as a crux of contrary forces.

The face is no longer invisible because it would disintegrate as an image but because it is caressed or touched, because it abandons itself to a sensibility that does not turn into perception. The ethical relation, transcendence, and alterity can then only be established between bodies, redefined here as nodal unities of a face and a skin. It is precisely because the face is a body in this sense that it cannot be seen and that it escapes images, according to Levinas. My relation to the neighbor is undergone as an immediate contact, a "leap over images" (*OB*, 72). Hence the third disengagement, which implies that subjects are always already bodies or flesh—not even *in* bodies or *in* flesh. It is the corporeality of the subject that renders it sensible to the Other. Incarnation is pre-original.[44]

43. Many other formulations emphasize the "crux" [*noeud*] formed henceforth by the face and the "skin," their homogeneity and even their "unity" (*OB*, 89–90).

44. Incarnation—unintelligible because prior to consciousness (*OB*, 79)—is not the Christian incarnation of a double nature, the intromission of a Verb in a body, a visibility of the invisible ("Anyone who has seen me has seen the Father," John 14:9). For Levinas, to be incarnated does not mean to be *in* the flesh, but *of* the flesh.

4. Consequently, the Other is no longer given in the heart of a "relation," a concept stemming from formal logic and a rationality of consciousness. A body-to-body no longer restricted to Eros, ethics, or the one-for-the-other, is experienced as "proximity." The excess proper to all contact forbids its objectification in a term-to-term relation,[45] and thereby forbids the emergence of any image: "The proximity of beings of flesh and blood is not their presence 'in the flesh [*en chair en et os*],' is not the fact that they take form for a gaze, presenting an exterior—quiddities, forms, offering images, which the eye absorbs" (*OB*, 78). This is the fourth escape.

THE PERSISTENCE OF IMAGES

The insistence with which Levinas underscores the separation between the body and the image illustrates how much the latter chases the body ever further, like its shadow or double, how much the image resists. Now, only this separation justifies the consideration of ethics as first philosophy, and it alone enables us to distinguish the holy from the sacred. According to Levinas's distinction,[46] images are sacred, they are not holy. They entertain one's curiosity for the divine, they cultivate the *libido videndi* and distract, whereas the truth of God is my neighbor. If the body were the producer of images, if the image were the continuation of the very movement whereby the body is made body—if figuration took root in a body where the gaze and the sexual organ were joined together—then this distinction between the holy and the sacred, between the truth of the religious and its staging [*mise en scène*], would be blurred.[47] And yet, once again we would be tempted to attribute to figuration what Levinas says about the other's body. By showing how the image pursues the body, how it is ultimately its secretion, we will clarify the difference that exists between figuration and simple image-representation. Let us review point by point the path Levinas takes:

1. The notion of the trace that Levinas employs to save the face from representation, or sight [*l'aspect*], paradoxically draws it even closer to

45. "Proximity does not congeal into a structure except when, *represented* in the demand for justice (which is reversible), it reverts to a simple relation" (*OB*, 82, emphasis added).

46. Levinas, *From the Sacred to the Holy*, in *Nine Talmudic Readings*, trans. Annette Aronowicz (Bloomington: Indiana University Press, 1990), especially the third reading.

47. Levinas asks the question: "How can holiness be confused with the sacred and turn into sorcery?" (*NTR*, 146).

figuration: figuration here is the image insofar as it is fabricated, urged to come, and traced, not insofar as it presents itself or represents. It is this urging (drive, compulsion) and this dynamic that are on the point of shattering form yet always retain it. With the trace, we leave the theoretical model of the image-representation but only to adopt that of the drawing: "The trace is sketched out and effaced in the face" (*OB*, 12).[48] A drawing is never complete, it refers to an absence that we cannot catch up to or "track down." We can always touch it up or make another go at it, but it opens onto an irretrievable absence. And yet it is, or rather it comes, presents itself as a passage, a route.

2. The diachronic relation to the face recalls, then, that a drawing is not the imprint of a past perception that once was present. The drawing, which is not opposed here to painting but to representation and is therefore identified with figuration itself, refers to a more distant past than anything that can be recollected,[49] to an immemoriality, to the "past of the Other where eternity is *delineated*" (*CPP*, 106, emphasis added), as Levinas states with respect to the face. It is with the Christian, pictorial term of "visitation" that Levinas describes the unexpected arrival [*survenue*] of the face in the world, the entry of a time from before birth into the heart of recuperable time.[50]

3. The unity of a face and a sexual organ in a body, which enables proximity, puts into question the meaning of *inversion*, the term used in *Totality and Infinity* to denote the link and the distance established between the face and the erotic body, on the one hand, and Eros and the work of art, on the other. Now, if inversion is conceived of as a unity, the beautiful work, the work of art—an inversion of the "feminine," but also already an image—is joined to the body from which it issues: "Proximity also *delineates* the trope of lyricism: to love by telling one's love to the beloved—love songs, the possibility of poetry, of art" (*OB*, 199, n.10, emphasis added). Beauty—what touches and moves—is given to a sensibility or a vulnerability and not, in a representation, to consciousness. The work of art is thus not what I judge to be beautiful

48. Or again: "It is this situation at first purely dialectical and quasi-verbal . . . that the exceptional signifyingness of the trace *delineates* [*dessine*] in the world" (*CPP*, 106, emphasis added).

49. "Painting opens onto itself, which opens onto the immemorial: the presence always- already and always- still there, inexhaustibly withdrawn in itself, tirelessly exposed before us" (Jean-Luc Nancy, *Visitation (de la peinture chrétienne)* [Paris: Galilée, 2001], 42).

50. See Nancy, *Visitation*, 52, where this expression of Levinas's is glossed in direct relation to its pictorial and Christian sense.

(as in Kant) nor what can become the object of an experience (as in Husserlian phenomenology), but "what comes near" because it comes from afar. "What comes near" is at once what must be approached and what approaches me.

4. With "proximity," Levinas can show that from Me to the Other there is not a relation between two terms, but a contact: the contact of "Saying," that is, a contact with the face itself, a contact that in its definition does not imply any contiguity. Consequently, I do not see the Other *if to see is to perceive*. But since the contact at issue here is not that of a hand against skin but that which is produced between his face and my eye, contact is also sustained within the heart of the gaze. In the end, only perception is excluded from vision, but not the touching of two vulnerabilities stripped of their form: "One can see and hear as one touches" (*OB*, 191, n. 9). It is with this type of vision that I see the face, and it is through it that contact becomes alterity: "In every vision contact is announced: sight and hearing caress the visible and the audible. Contact is not an openness upon being, but an exposure to being" (*OB*, 80). What gives itself to be seen is not exhausted in representation: as trace, drawing, figuration, it addresses itself to a sensibility and a susceptibility.

FIGURATION

Levinas insists on excluding the image, and the image resists in the form of figuration. While he claims to suppress the image, Levinas frees himself only from representation. Why, then, does he continue to talk about images? To preserve the possibility of a holiness that would not "be confused with the sacred and turn into sorcery," the possibility of a formlessness that would not be tempted to re-form itself. But this possibility is never established: the image is continually reborn of the body like the head of a monster, of a *monstrum*. It remains an ambiguity, that of the intact, the pure, the non-contaminated.[51] Figuration is the nec-

---

51. Derrida has noted the unity of the holy and the sacred, while also remarking upon the perhaps necessary attempt to distinguish between them: "We will have to devote all our attention to this series, taking as our point of departure this last word (*heilig*), this German word whose semantic history seems however to resist the rigorous dissociation that Levinas wishes to maintain between a natural, 'pagan,' even Graeco-Christian sacredness, and the holiness of (Jewish) law, before or under Roman religion" ("Faith and Knowledge: The Two Sources of 'Religion' at the Limits of Reason Alone," trans. Samuel Weber, in Derrida, *Acts of Religion*, ed. Gil Anidjar [New York: Routledge, 2002], 54 [trans. mod.]).

essary secretion of a body that is at once face and sexual organ, and thus not a homogeneous substance able to receive meaning from conscious experience [*un vécu de conscience*], but a gap between the two, between a high and a low, a holiness and a sacredness. What body are we talking about?

A body is never alone: humanity begins with two, in a body-to-body[52]—the face-to-face and the caress—from which the image as figure is born. Figuration finds its necessity here. Or, to put it differently, there is no ethical/erotic experience that does not initiate a movement toward figuration, be it the weakest or most banal of inclinations. Factual contingencies complicate these questions of degree. But art is already announced in the relation to the Other by virtue of a *compulsion to figure*. With this term, I wish to stress at once the role of drives in artistic activity and the ontological constraint that sustains this activity. The ethical and erotic origin of figuration does not imply that there are two distinct sources that would add up or be mutually articulated, nor that on an injunction from the Other a psychological motivation would be superimposed. The source of the work of art is one, but double, the drive being already—unlike an instinct—turned toward alterity. The propensity to figure is therefore at once—but without schism—ethical and erotic: desire and obedience.

Against this compulsion to figure we could easily object that, by lack of either talent or desire, not all people devote themselves to figural activity. Even if this were true, however, nothing here would be put into question: the image comes wherever there is a body developing itself: in children, for instance, where we would undoubtedly find few exceptions. But also on a supra-individual level: when the individual enters a new body, the social body, he or she can delegate this compulsion—to artists, to churches, to technicians. It is, then, in this community that the necessity of figuration is manifest: there is no social body that has not compulsively produced images, any more than there is a child who has not extended lived alterity by figuring it.

—Translated by Nicole Simek and Zahi Zalloua

52. "I am bound to others before being bound to my body" (*OB*, 76).

EDITH WYSCHOGROD

Levinas's Other and the Culture of the Copy

> To an ever-increasing degree, the work of art reproduced becomes the reproduction of a work of art designed for reproducibility. From a photographic negative, for example, one can make any number of prints; to ask for the "authentic" print makes no sense.
> —Walter Benjamin, "The Work of Art in the Age of its Technical Reproducibility"

> The consciousness of representation lies in knowing that the object is not there. The perceived elements are not the object but are like its "old garments." . . . [I]n the absence of the object they do not force its presence, but by their presence insist on its absence. . . . They . . . mark its removal, as though the represented object . . . were disincarnated in its own reflection.
> —Emmanuel Levinas, "Reality and Its Shadow"

> The movie ["The Matrix"] portrays a Baudrillardian future in which tyrannical, hyper-intelligent machines have enslaved the human race and connected all the humans by cables to a computer matrix where they live in a virtual reality. . . . The "real world" . . . appears almost not at all.
> —Brent Staples, *The New York Times*, 24 May 2002

When objects of perception or cognition are said to be the same, what is generally meant is that a trait or traits of an object can be found in one or more other objects. A resemblance between or among them is predicated with respect to those traits that are repeated despite otherwise diverse attributes. That by virtue of which an object is said to resemble another can be interpreted either as a preexistent form or as an essence inferred from observed qualitative or quantitative properties. Not only may forms or essences be thought to express what is exemplified in objects that are envisaged as their instantiations, but they may be viewed as the origin of that sameness, as imbued with generative power even if this origin is constituted as such only after the fact. Otherness is determined as the absence of a common trait, essence, or form.

YFS 104, *Encounters with Levinas,* ed. Thomas Trezise, © 2004 by Yale University.

More recently, these accounts of same and other encrypted in the history of metaphysics have been reinscribed in linguistic terms. Language is seen not as representing what is prior to itself but as a code embodying conventions that render repeatability possible, conventions of iterability that enable one to say the same. Or, if we fast forward to a recent description of what is meant by organization in biological life, we find the logic of iterability thus described replicated in the claim that, for such organization to be possible, sameness is intrinsic to "those relations that must exist among the components of a system for it to be a member of a specific class."[1]

The meaning of the same can also be understood in accordance with Husserl's phenomenological principle that objects are disclosed as objects for a consciousness that reaches out to or intends them. Not only are objects subject to the conditions of their disclosure—in that regard in accordance with Kant's transcendental account of cognition—but the being of what is disclosed, of the phenomenon, is subordinate to an intentional consciousness that reasserts itself in all cognitive and perceptual acts. When exteriority is attributed to objects, it is an exteriority determined by the interiority that reveals it, an outside that cannot be other than an outside that is inside. There is no *Ding an sich* apart from the phenomenon as brought to light by a self-identical consciousness.

For Emmanuel Levinas, this epistemological account poses an ethical question. Even in the absence of a reflective awareness of its operations as coercive, the intentionality of consciousness can be perceived as a mechanism of control that subverts otherness, specifically the otherness of other persons, and, as such, is always already guilty of a certain violence. If the sublation of what is other is to be circumvented, there must be that which cannot become content and which transcends the capacity of consciousness to contain it, an excess that cannot become the aim of an intending act. Such an excess would provide a disconnect, as it were, a disempowering of the consciousness seeking to encompass it. Does the inapprehensibility of this excess, its resistance to description, render it meaningless, or can it be argued that the descriptive and logical properties of language fail to exhaust the uses of language, that in its performative capacity, language solicits and com-

---

1. Humberto R. Maturana and Francisco Varela, *The Tree of Knowledge: The Biological Roots of Human Understanding* (Boston: New Science Library, 1987), 47; as cited in N. Katherine Hayles, *How We Became Posthuman: Virtual Bodies in Cybernetics, Literature, and Informatics* (Chicago: University of Chicago Press, 1999), 152.

mands? Is language not always already an address to and from another who cannot be contained within a common genus, an essence of the "human"? The other as absolute exteriority contests the power of consciousness to reduce it to the same.

I hope to put Levinas's notions of same and other to the test by considering their possible destabilization in a culture of the copy in which the distinction between original and replica is undermined. Can his account of the same as that which is contested by an other whose descriptor is simply that it is otherwise than being be sustained and, if not, must the other, the condition of ethics, not also be affected? I shall turn first to the Levinasian subject, for whom repetition is lived as re-identification and re-creation of the self, of an ipseity that is a precondition for cognition. I shall then examine some widely disseminated views of gene replication and a theory of artificial life that undermine his description of ipseity, before considering Levinas's view of fecundity as the reproduction of oneself in one's progeny and Kierkegaard's analysis of repetition in relation to the time of ipseity. Finally, I will suggest how Chilean biologists Humberto R. Maturana and Francisco Varela, who interpret replication in terms of the recursiveness within autonomous living systems, can be seen to offer some surprising prospects for effecting an accommodation with the Levinasian account of the subject.

SOME PRELIMINARIES: CONSCIOUSNESS AND THE CORPOREAL I

What can be meant by Levinas's astonishing claim that "alterity is possible only starting from *me*" (*TI*, 40)? Does he not insist that the absolute exteriority of the other cannot be brought into a relation of correlation with the consciousness that intends it without impairing its alterity? Even if *ex hypothesi* the relation of correlation is one in which the self and the other are not reciprocal terms, he cautions that the relata might still be incorporated into a system open to an observer outside itself. More important, even if an unbridgeable distance or exteriority determines the meaning of otherness, Levinas concedes that alterity cannot be hermetically sealed, cordoned off from that which renders it other. Thus otherness is, in a crucial sense, dependent upon the same.

The reduction of exteriority by consciousness is contingent upon what is prior to it, the same produced as an egoism that enters into a relation with the other (*TI*, 38). Levinas avers: "The alterity, the radical heterogeneity of the Other, is possible only if the Other is other with respect to a term whose essence is to remain at the point of departure, to serve as *entry* into the relation, to be the Same not relatively but absolutely. *A term can remain absolutely at the point of departure of the relation only as I*" (*TI*, 36, emphasis in original). To be I is neither to be as a sequence of alterations reborn at every instant nor as an unchanging essence but rather as that which reidentifies itself in its embracing of the heterogeneous content it thinks and represents. What is more, and in conformity with Husserl's phenomenological account, the I bends back upon itself and, in this self-apprehension, overcomes its first naïveté.

Yet in accord with Heidegger's account of the Dasein of *Being and Time,* the Levinasian subject is not a thought-monad, an I that merely represents itself to itself, but an I that is embedded in a concrete system of world relations. For Levinas, world is not a hostile environment but the place in which one can be at home with oneself. Home (primordially, if not in fact) is an enabling site in which one dwells and that allows for the freedom of work and possession. The otherness intrinsic to world relations should not be confused with the relation to the other person, who is unlike the nexus of objects among which one lives and that are simply exterior to oneself. The other cannot be located at a site. Yet even if the "*sway* [*pouvoir*] of the I will not cross the distance marked by the alterity of the other" (*TI*, 38), must we not ask whether the distance and height that separate me from the other can be envisaged otherwise than spatially? Even if the relation of same and other is enacted as language, still "the Same gathered up in its ipseity as an 'I,' as a particular existent unique and autochthonous" (*TI*, 39) must go out of itself toward the other. If the command of the other is to refrain from harming her/him, the other cannot be a gnostic subject but must be a body that exists in a world even if this location cannot be pinpointed across an inviolable space.

In elaborating upon what is meant by life as bodily existence, Levinas asserts: "Life is a body, not only a lived body where its self-sufficiency emerges, but a crossroads of physical forces, a body-effect." Yet, he continues, "there is no duality between lived body and physical body. The world life acquires . . . is also the physical world." The relation of life with that which it inhabits is lived as a freedom that is "a by-product of life" (*TI*, 164–65). Bodily existence exhibits both self-mastery and dependence upon what is not itself, the environment in which it dwells and works. Through dwelling and work, the self experiences a sense of security over and against its awareness of the death that is to come, a doubleness lived as a postponement of death and, as such, as the dimension of time. It is this rift at the heart of corporeal existence that is consciousness. For Levinas, consciousness is life's temporality, disincarnate, lived as postponement or having time, as attempting to ward off what threatens one's existence.

To exist as forestalling danger is to will. The body's actions do not, however, follow a preordained goal but are corporeal engagements involved in a process of self-modification. For Levinas, the active self recreates itself along the way, both "seeking and *catching hold* of the goal, with all the contingencies this involves" (*TI*, 167). What is more, the being that acts is one that consciously represents itself as acting. Yet representation is disingenuous, "claim[ing] to substitute itself *after the fact* for this life in reality, so as to constitute this very reality" (*TI*, 169). Representation itself is not merely a negation derived dialectically from relations of the living being to its environment, but an absolutely new event. It is a withdrawal that is lived as entering into relation with another human being encountered as a human face. The face that calls the I into question, Levinas insists, is language (*TI*, 171). It is as a relation to the other that language is first an ethical event that makes possible the offering of a world to another. But "[l]anguage, far from presupposing universality and generality, first makes them possible. Language presupposes interlocutors, a plurality" (*TI*, 73).

CLONING IPSEITY

It can be argued that the body that acts, that is a point of world orientation or exists as a sensate subject has been undercut by the claims of those evolutionary biologists who redesign the body of ordinary experience to become quintessentially coded information. In the most radical accounts, such as that of Richard Dawkins, the relation of the form of the organism, the phenomenological body, is engaged in ever more tenuous relations with the germ-line, a powerfully active biological entity that is both an agent and a recipient of the body's actions.

Dawkins does not deny that the phenotype (an organism's manifest characteristics) is the result of the interaction of genetic makeup and environment. But for Dawkins, phenotype and genes are not inseparable in that the outcomes of gene activity may lie outside the bodies in which the genes are lodged. Thus, an entity made up exclusively of

genes is extended beyond the organism that the genes inhabit to constitute a new individual. The gene's eye view of evolution sees evolution as taking place not on behalf of the organism as an indivisible
living unit but rather in the interest of the gene, that "little bit of
chromosome which potentially lasts for many generations."[2] Now,
modes of inheritance heretofore ascribed to organisms are attributed to
genes.

To make sense of this contention, it is crucial to see the centrality
of replication in Dawkins's account of the gene's operations.[3] It is in
the interest of reproducing itself, the gene, rather than the phenotype,
that natural selection takes place. For Dawkins, a replicator is anything
of which copies can be made. Information bearing DNA molecules,
gene strings, are replicators, active when their effects lead to their being copied, passive when they die out. For Dawkins, the gene is the
"unit of heredity" that is retained in the evolutionary process. Only
those likely to be copied survive while passive replicators become ex-
tinct (*Extended Phenotype*, 82–85). This account is complicit with
Dawkins's famous claim that "a predominant quality to be expected in
a successful gene is ruthless selfishness. This gene selfishness will usually give rise to selfishness in individual behavior" (*Selfish Gene*, 2).
What remains clear is that while the phenotype continues to be an "in-
strument of replicator preservation," it is not itself preserved but
"works as a unit for the preservation and propagation of . . . replicators"
(*Extended Phenotype*, 114); or, as he states more graphically, "A body
is the genes' way of preserving the genes unaltered" (*Selfish Gene*, 25).
Dawkins maintains that his radical stance is not taken to support the
truth of particular factual propositions but rather to open a way of looking at new facts and ideas (*Selfish Gene*, 1).

Levinas does not, so far as I know, discuss the meaning of genes
as replicators. Surprisingly, however, in the essay "Reality and Its
Shadow," he develops a notion of resemblance operative in the gener-

---

2. Richard Dawkins, *The Selfish Gene* (New York: Oxford University Press, 1976),
35. This work is more radical in its claims for the longevity and selfishness of genes than
the later *The Extended Phenotype*.

3. Dawkins, *The Extended Phenotype: The Gene as the Unit of Selection* (Oxford:
W. H. Freeman and Company, 1982), 81–96. I consider the relation of gene and pheno-
type described in this paragraph in relation to Neoplatonism in my article "From
Neoplatonism to Souls in Silico: Quests for Immortality," in *Rethinking Philosophy of
Religion: Approaches from Continental Philosophy*, ed. Philip Goodchild (New York:
Fordham University Press, 2002), 260.

ating of images in art that may lend itself to reinscription in the context of gene replication. In contrast to signs or words, which are transparent toward their objects, images refer to objects by way of resemblance. But resemblance is not, as Plato would have it, a relation of original to copy but rather the very movement that engenders the image. "Reality would not be only what it is, what it is disclosed to be in truth, but also its double, its shadow, its image. Being is not only itself, it escapes itself " (*CPP*, 6). Because a being does not coincide with itself, there is that which remains behind the being, something that withdraws from it. Thus, there is a duality in a being that both is what it is and also something estranged from itself. It is this relationship between a being and its image that *is* resemblance (*CPP*, 6).

To be sure, unlike genes, images are visible. Yet Dawkins's interpretation of gene string and phenotype repeats in its context the ontological relation of reality and image, in that for Levinas "by the simple fact of becoming an image, [the represented object] is converted into a non-object; the image as such enters into categories proper to it. . . . The disincarnation of reality by the image is not equivalent to a simple diminution in degree" (*CPP*, 5). The ontology of images provides an unintentional blueprint for the relation of gene string to phenotype in that, like the Levinasian image, genes occupy the place of the object "as though the represented object died, were degraded, were disincarnated in its own reflection" (*CPP*, 7).

THE PROGENY WHO IS AND IS NOT ME

It is not surprising to find that evolutionary biology is focused upon the modus operandi of reproduction. It is, however, startling to see that, for Levinas, intrinsic to the self that is open to the other, there is a conatus to replicate itself, a movement in which the self relates itself to its future through a relation to the beloved, a relation he calls fecundity. Thus Levinas writes: "Infinite being, that is, ever recommencing being—which could not bypass subjectivity, for it could not recommence without it—is produced in the guise of fecundity" (*TI*, 268). The birth of a child seen as the outcome of an erotic encounter is not a continuation of one's own possibilities, but a link with a future that one does not control. In the relations of consciousness and world, the I reiterates itself. One's child is, however, a duality within that which is identical rather than a falling back into or reiterating of oneself. The child is not an extension of an I who would ensure its identity in reembodiments, "avatars" of oneself, yet the child is one's own future despite its discontinuity with oneself (*TI*, 268).

That, for Levinas, the child is the son and woman the biological agent of the reproductive process is open to (and has received) warranted criticism. What is more, new reproductive technologies call into question the scenario of eros that Levinas depicts. But it is the telos or goal of reproduction that is most deeply challenged by Dawkins's version of neo-Darwinism. Replication is not in the service of another who is and is not oneself, nor even undertaken in the interest of perpetuating the species or the individual organism as the unit of natural selection. Replication seeks to conserve the active germ replicator that is, for Dawkins, "the ancestor of an indefinitely long line of descendant replicators" (*Extended Phenotype*, 83). Replicants expand power, that of the germ line, by virtue of a sheer increase in the number of copies. Although some germ lines may die out, "any germ-line replicator is *potentially* immortal" (*Extended Phenotype*, 83).

The interpretation of the gene as code lends itself readily to the modelling of artificial life, life that is humanly contrived, through the use of computational prototypes. Richard Dawkins approvingly cites D'Arcy Thompson's claim that "any animal form can be turned into a related form by a mathematical transformation, although it is not obvious that the transformation will be a simple one" (*Extended Phenotype*, 2). In present-day continuity with this prototype, Stephen Wolfram writes: "[T]hinking in terms of programs is . . . even more obvious for biological systems than for physical ones. For in a physical system the rules of a program must normally be deduced indirectly from the laws of physics. But in a biological organism there is genetic material which can be thought of quite directly as providing a program for the development of the organism."[4]

In turning to computational paradigms not merely to comprehend but to create life, artificial life theorist Christopher Langton asserts that life is not a property of matter but rather of its organization, for which computational models are eminently suited. Now, research can be directed "from the *mechanics* of life to the *logic* of life."[5] Langton contends that more can be learned from the "creation of life *in silico*" than could be learned by relying on the organic chemicals of carbon-

4. Stephen Wolfram, *A New Kind of Science* (Champaign, IL: Wolfram Media, Inc., 2002), 383.

5. Christopher G. Langton, "Artificial Life," in *The Philosophy of Artificial Life*, ed. Margaret A. Boden (New York: Oxford University Press, 1996), 47.

chain chemistry, in that computational models open up the "space of *possible* life" ("Artificial Life," 50). In effect, what is being sought is the generating of behavior through the creation of computational automata.

It has been thought that computers can only do what their programs enable them to do but cannot generate mutations or novel animal behavior. However, it is now claimed that, if sufficiently powerful, computers can transcend their programs and are inherently unpredictable. Langton contends that "it is impossible in the general case to determine *any* non-trivial property of the future behavior of a sufficiently powerful computer from a mere inspection of its program and its initial state alone. . . . [T]he only way to find out anything . . . is to start the system up and watch what happens" ("Artificial Life," 58). For Stephen Wolfram, nature itself may be thought of as a universal computer that generates complexity from simple programs, a claim that can be supported by allowing the programs to keep on running.

ANSWERING BACK I: DESTABILIZING THE I

Can Levinas's account of representation as "a determination of the Other by the Same without the Same being determined by the Other" (*TI*, 170) and his description of ipseity as a passive unitary self accommodate some of the conceptual moves embedded in theories of germline replication and artificial life? It could be argued that Heidegger's critique of calculative thinking as revealing the meaning of being and his account of enframing as the manifestation of being as will could in effect discredit the ontological underpinnings of artificial life theorists. Had Heidegger not already referred to cybernetics as the metaphysics of the atomic age? It could, however, be countered that Heidegger's critique of cybernetics could not be applied to Darwin's depiction of evolution as involving living systems. But Heidegger contends that Darwin's model of nature is itself one of instrumentality. As Keith Ansell Pearson points out, for Darwin "artifice [is] the common factor in the technical evolution of both nature and human breeding . . . [a view] conditioned by considerations of utility."[6] Utility governs the process. For Heidegger, by contrast and in conformity with biologist Jacob van Uexküll's claims, the animal from whom we are said to evolve inhab-

6. Keith Ansell Pearson, *Viroid Life: Perspectives on Nietzsche and the Transhuman Condition* (London: Routledge, 1997), 113.

its a phenomenal world, an *Umwelt*, but unlike humans is "poor in world" (Pearson, *Viroid Life*, 118).

The picture of evolution criticized by Heidegger presupposes a closed universe, one that could not have taken into account Langton's and Wolfram's newly conceived views of artificial life (commonly referred to as A-life) alluded to earlier. Could its "bottom-up processes of spontaneous self-organization" (Pearson, *Viroid Life*, 183), an open universe in which conditions of uncertainty prevail, provide a toehold for the Levinasian same? In consonance with this view, Pearson, citing biologist Gilbert Simondon, notes that the becoming of a biological system must be seen as a metastable equilibrium. "A being does not possess a 'unity in its identity,' which would be that of a stable state in which transformation is not possible, but rather it enjoys a *"transductive unity,'* meaning that it is able to pass out of phase with itself" (*Viroid Life*, 183–84). Becoming as a temporal process does not simply fall upon a pre-existing stable entity. Instead, time is invented in accordance with this process of ontogenetic change.

Can the Levinasian notion of ipseity open the way for establishing a certain compatibility between Simondon's "metastable equilibrium" and the repetition intrinsic to ipseity? In his crucial essay, "Substitution," Levinas maintains: "The identity of ipseity is not due to any kind of distinguishing characteristic . . . like fingerprints, and which as a principle of individuation would win for this identity a proper name. . . . The identity of the 'oneself' is not the inertia of an individuated quiddity. . . . The identity of the *oneself* is not equivalent to the identity of identification" (*BPW*, 84). A separated being that reidentifies itself in this way is not one who is in a stable state but a being that remembers, one whose mode of temporalization is recursive. In consonance with this view of ipseity, Levinas writes in a key passage of *Totality and Infinity:* "The cause of being is thought or known by its effect *as though* it were posterior to its effect. . . . The posteriority of the anterior—an inversion logically absurd—is produced . . . only by memory or by thought. . . . [T]he *After* or the *Effect* conditions the *Before* or the *Cause*" (*TI*, 54). The affirmation that memory reverses the ongoingness of the historical order of time is especially significant in that the post hoc constitution of the origin destabilizes the self as identical with itself. If this claim is accepted, how is the self that recreates itself to be understood?

I cannot hope briefly to engage the complex relation of Levinas to

Kierkegaard but rather, in a brief excursus, to consider some crucial configurations of recursiveness in Kierkegaard that wend their way errantly through Levinas's account of the self-repetition of ipseity.[7] In Kierkegaard's work, *Repetition* (not mentioned by Levinas in this context), recollection and repetition are seen from the vantage point of the problematic figure of Kierkegaard's pseudonymous author.[8] It is Constantin Constantius who declares that, whereas the Greeks saw knowledge as recollection, modern philosophy sees it as repetition. "Repetition and recollection are the same movement, only in opposite directions; for what is recollected has been, is repeated backwards, whereas repetition properly so-called is recollected forwards."[9] If repetition is possible, he declares, happiness is its psychological outcome, whereas the outcome of recollection is unhappiness. Repetition does not demand novelty "but it requires courage to will repetition" (*Repetition,* 5). Is the time of repetition thus understood not the lived time of Levinas's separated self at home with itself? The happy individual, according to Kierkegaard, is one for whom "repetition is a task for freedom . . . [and] signifies freedom itself."[10] One who wills repetition seeks neither perpetual novelty nor the mere preservation of the past. Could it perhaps be argued without unduly stretching the point that recollecting forward is an apt figure for determining the future behavior of a computational system not from an inspection of a program's initial state but by running the program?

ANSWERING BACK II: THE RECURSIVENESS OF THE OBSERVER

Is it possible to find in the culture of the copy, in which life is configured as code, the reflexivity of consciousness as it is usually understood by phenomenology? Jean-Pierre Dupuy asks whether representation

---

7. There are a number of references to Kierkegaard in the Levinas corpus. Pertinent to the present context is his positive view of Kierkegaard's account of the desire for God. See "Hermeneutics and Beyond," in *OG,* 109. Also worth noting is his claim that "the Kierkegaardian God is not simply the bearer of certain attributes of humility; he is a way of truth . . . not determined by the phenomenon" ("Enigma and Phenomenon," *BPW,* 71).

8. See Edward F. Mooney, "*Repetition:* Getting the World Back," in *The Cambridge Companion to Kierkegaard,* ed. Alastair Hannay and Gordon D. Marino (Cambridge: Cambridge University Press, 1998).

9. Søren Kierkegaard, *Repetition: An Essay in Experimental Psychology,* trans. Walter Lowrie (Princeton: Princeton University Press, 1941), 3–4.

10. Quoted by Mooney, "*Repetition,*" 294, from "Selected Entries from Kierkegaard's Journals and Papers Pertaining to *Repetition.*"

and the transcendental dimension of cognition have been altogether eliminated from meaningful discourse by epistemologies grounded in computation and physical laws.[11] Is it possible to reinscribe the reflexivity of phenomenological consciousness in new terms? Can the role of the observer in self-regulating living systems go proxy, as it were, for that of consciousness?

If phenomenology's account of intentionality can be naturalized, perhaps the best prospects for its reinscription lie in the study of closed autonomous and dynamic living systems as developed in the Chilean school of autopoiesis. According to this group of biologists, changes in a living system (such as that of neural networks) are the result of the system's own activity. External events occur as perturbations of the system that acquire meaning only as a result of the network's own activity. Humberto R. Maturana and Francisco Varela, founders of the school, maintain that thought does not emanate from a Cartesian *cogito* that guarantees its truth but emerges from the organization of living systems as self-making or self-producing. Maturana (upon whose thought I shall focus) is concerned not with the promise of meaning and truth but rather with the mechanisms or processes that enable living systems to operate successfully.[12]

In Maturana's work, "Cognition," the observer is not seen as extrinsic to the operation of living systems but is built into its explanation, defined as the modelling of the system by a "beholder."[13] The designation of a thing as a unity depends upon the observer's stipulation of a distinction between an entity that may be simple or complex and its background. It is only complex entities that exhibit both structure, the components that constitute an entity as of a type or class, and organization, the relation among its components that generates the dy-

11. See Jean-Pierre Dupuy, *The Mechanization of the Mind*, trans. M. B. DeBevoise (Princeton: Princeton University Press, 2000), 102–107.

12. Humberto R. Maturana, "Cognition," in *Wahrnehmung und Kommunikation*, ed. Peter M. Hejl, Wolfram K. Köck, and Gerhard Roth (Frankfurt: Peter Lang, 1978), 29–49. See http://www.enolagaia.com/M78bCog.html, 30–31/4–5. Notes cite the online reprinted translation; original page numbers are followed by page numbers of the online document.

13. Katherine Hayles, in *How We Became Posthuman*, points out that the early work of Maturana and Varela allows for construing the metadomain of the observer as though it were a separate entity, whereas in the later work the observers are integral to the network of processes that produced them (145–46). In a perceptive analysis of the autopoietic school, Mark C. Taylor tracks the Hegelian implications of its account of the complexity of living systems. See his *The Moment of Complexity* (Chicago: University of Chicago Press, 2001), esp. 92–93.

namics of complex entities. As unities, entities belong to a domain or space in which they can be distinguished. The autonomy of unities as autopoietic systems is what Maturana calls "structure-specified" in that other entities merely trigger changes that are essentially determined by their intrinsic structure ("Cognition," 32/6). In sum, for Maturana, living systems belong to "a class of systems each member of which is defined as a composite unity (system), as a network of productions of components which . . . through their interactions recursively constitute and realize the network of productions that produced them" ("Cognition," 33/8).

In Levinas's view, the self, which is at first immersed in an environment he calls the elemental, closes off a part of that environment from which it then distinguishes itself so that it exists as a separated being. The space it inhabits, what Maturana would call its domain, is for Levinas the dwelling or the home. To be sure, the I, the self or ipseity that is prior to the self at home with itself is, as we have seen, the accusatory self of responsibility that renders the self answerable for "everything and everyone." Yet this self is also a unity that is "its own content," a unity out of phase with the rhythms of life that lie outside it (*BPW*, 85–86). The reflexivity of this ipseity that passively folds back upon itself, that makes possible the self's relations to exteriority, the reduction of the other to the same, is reflected in Maturana's account of the reflexive unity of self-maintaining living systems as they respond to external perturbations. For Levinas, the recursiveness of the same emerges in all of its reflexivity as "the return of being to itself as knowledge" and is produced at the "fulcrum" of an ipseity that "is" as a non-essence or non-quiddity that cannot yet be encapsulated in language (*BPW*, 85).

It is significant that, for Maturana, even if living systems are independent, they are not alone. Systems are structurally coupled with others of a similar type or class, a coupling that is a precondition for establishing what he calls a "consensual domain" in which linguistic distinctions proliferate, piggy-backing, as it were, upon one another. In Maturana's arcane formulation: "When this recursive consensual domain is established an observer sees a generative linguistic domain in which metadescriptions take place. A linguistic domain with such characteristics is a *language*" ("Cognition," 43/22). Although, for Levinas, the other does not first appear to the self in the language of concepts but is experienced as the pressure of responsibility, nevertheless self and other are not coinhabitants of a space but share a world. It is as and through language that the world is designated to another: "The generality of the word institutes a common world. . . . Language does not exteriorize a representation preexisting in me: it puts in common a world hitherto mine. Language *effectuates* the entry of things into a new ether in which they receive a name and become concepts" (*TI*, 173–74).

But the question remains: who or what performs the function of the observer for Maturana and how is this observer related to phenomenological consciousness as understood by Levinas? For Maturana, behaviors are themselves already descriptions and recursions are metadescriptions. "When a metadomain of descriptions (or distinctions) is generated in a linguistic domain, the observer is generated. Or, in other words, to operate in a metalinguistic domain . . . is to be an observer" ("Cognition," 44/23). An infinite regress is precluded by the built-in limitations of a structure that allows the observer to define her position and to operate as if outside that structure.

To be sure, for Levinas, being determines its modes of being-given, thereby ordering the forms of knowledge that comprehend it. It is as the correlation of that which is and the consciousness that intends it, of the noema, the intentional object, and the noesis or intending act (in Husserl's terms), that being assures the possibility of a certain order of truth. What is crucial is that this relation requires a distinction between beings and the consciousness that brings them to light in accordance with its own laws (*OG*, 100–101). Thus, in addition to the rationality relative to the knowledge of beings, the rationality of evidence, there must be what Levinas calls a change in level or deepening that is obtained by turning to the subject that intends. "It is a question of awakening a life that evidence absorbed or made us forget or rendered anonymous. . . . [I]t is a question of descending from the entity illuminated in evidence toward the subject" (*OG*, 18). As ontological objects vary, different modes of consciousness are called into play. Levinas notes that in the first edition of Husserl's *Logical Investigations*, it is conceded that even in the realm of pure logic, the so-called "pure law," whose apodicticity is assured, can be filtered through "fluctuating verbal significations" (*OG*, 19) and that therefore an analysis of the psychic acts that intend them is required. "It is only through reflection upon the experience of consciousness that objective terms are maintained in an evidence that . . . awakens to itself only in reflection" (*OG*, 20).

Since Maturana speaks not of reflective consciousness but of observers who are living systems, are we not fully determined by the built-in limitations of these systems as autopoietic unities and by the pre-established parameters of their structural couplings? Yet it must not be forgotten that the world of the observer is one of language. *"Everything that is said is said by an observer to another observer that could be himself"* ("Cognition," 30/4, emphasis in original). We as observers can escape from the ways in which structural couplings determine our actions in that "our operation in a linguistic domain . . . allows us to generate a metadomain of descriptions" ("Cognition," 48/28). Maturana speaks of thinking, a recursive circling within neurophysiological processes, and of linguistic metadomains, rather than of the emergence of consciousness. What is crucial, however, is that we can arrive from thinking to what functions as self-consciousness through language. As Katherine Hayles notes: "The observer generates self-consciousness . . . when he endlessly describes himself describing himself" (*How We Became Posthuman,* 144–45). Does the reflexivity of the observer as self-generated metadescription not reinscribe what phenomenological inquiry claims to derive as an achievement of the transcendental reduction, the being of consciousness?

What is significant for Levinas are the ethical as well as the epistemic implications of this reduction. In consonance with the received view, he notes that, in *Ideas I,* Husserl questions the trustworthiness of naive evidence and, without repudiating the data of consciousness, initiates a suspension of belief in the existence of the world so that a phenomenon can emerge for consciousness in its essential nature. For Levinas, this account highlights an ambiguity in Husserl's thought that provides an entering wedge for his own new way of configuring the other. Husserl's aim, the preservation of the claims of intuition as the guarantor of certainty, is perpetually placed in question by the transcendental reduction. Yet this placing in question is for Levinas not a loss but a liberation from the ideal of adequation and from the hegemony of being.

In *Cartesian Meditations,* Husserl is seen to move further in the direction of a break with the ideal of apodicticity as grounded in adequation, for even if the *cogito sum* is given as indubitable, Levinas notes that transcendental experience itself is submitted to criticism (*OG,* 21–23).[14] The transcendental reduction, for Levinas, is to be interpreted as

---

14. Paul Ricoeur writes that in the first of the *Cartesian Meditations,* Husserl is "shifting the privilege of primary evidence from the presence of the world to the pres-

"a reflection upon reflection . . . a process without completion of the criticism of criticism." Thus, Levinas continues, criticism engenders an awakening of the subject to the "living presence of the I to itself" (*OG*, 22–23).[15] It is this reflexivity that opens the possibility for expanding the Levinasian account of the same to encompass Maturana's version of the recursiveness of living systems without endorsing the model of computational automata.

Maturana contends that, as inhabitants of consensual domains, we are not locked into "the closure of our individual autopoiesis" ("Cognition," 48/29). Because we are affected by and affect the lives of others, our conduct is inescapably ethical. What is more, Maturana warns, interactions that develop through structural couplings might enable totalitarian political systems to totally specify "the experiences of the human beings under [their] sway" ("Cognition," 48/28). At the same time, loving relations with others are possible. "Love," he contends, "is not blind because it does not negate, love accepts, and, therefore, is visionary" ("Cognition," 49/29). Similarly, for Levinas, individuals can become the bearers of forces that command them so that they derive their meaning from a social and historical totality. However, for Levinas, the ethical relation cannot be one of a love that is visionary in that vision reduces otherness to the same. What is more, for Maturana, the ethical relation is one of mirroring in that we learn to see ourselves and others as reciprocal reflections. For Levinas, meaning arises from the "diachronic foreignness of the other in my responsibility for him, [from] this 'difference among indiscernibles'—I and the other—without common genus . . . [from] a non-indifference in me for the other" (*OG*, 167). The ethical relation demands a radical diachrony of time that could resist the synchronic mode of structural coupling. The self for Levinas is opened to a meaning that is beyond what "each one's internal re-presentation signifies" and "beyond my perseverance in being" (*OG*, 166–67), a reflexivity that is drawn to but cannot internalize the other.

---

ence of the ego. This challenge to the pseudo-evidence (*Selbstverständlichkeit*) attaching to the presence of the world is the transcendental *epoché* itself [putting out of play or bracketing the existence of the world]." The belief in being is dispelled so that I gain the "for-me-ness of the world" (*Husserl: An Analysis of His Phenomenology*, trans. Lester Embree [Evanston, IL: Northwestern University Press, 1967], 87–88).

15. Levinas is quoting here from Edmond Husserl, *Méditations cartésiennes*, trans. Gabrielle Pfeiffer and Emmanuel Levinas (Paris: Vrin, 1969), 19.

IN/CONCLUSION

Is the Levinasian account of the same, understood as the reduction of exteriority by a consciousness that apprehends it, subverted by the culture of the copy as manifested in recent accounts of the activity of genes? And, if so, is an ethics based on the radical alterity of the other person not also undermined? Or does the Levinasian view of an ipseity that is prior to, and the condition for, ethics as well as for rational consciousness, offer grounds that both challenge and accommodate the culture of the copy? For Levinas, the starting point for thinking the same is bound up with the thinking of essence, a term that can be standardly understood as the guarantor of the sameness of its instantiations and as imbued with generative power. Thinking cannot occur apart from its relation to being but must think what Levinas calls the ess*a*nce of being, insisting that "we write 'ess*a*nce' with an '*a*' . . . to give a name to the verbal aspect of the word 'being.' " He goes on to say that "the experience of nameable beings and of *esse* itself is the result of . . . an experience of the fundamental . . . an ontological experience of the firmness of the earth." This fundament grounds his claim that "*experience of identity* or *experience of being qua being* are tautological" (*OG*, 112).

Levinas's account can hardly be rendered compatible with that of hard-line gene determinists or with those theorists for whom the self is an artifact of computational processes. In conformity with the former view, a gene-line is seen as having no rigid boundaries, as potentially immortal, and the purpose of natural selection as the preservation of the gene-line. Although Levinas does not comment specifically on such claims, there are surprising affinities between his description of the connection between reality and image and the relation of genes to visible bodies. Thus, his critique of the image may provide an entering wedge for a critical analysis of germ-line determinism.

The recursiveness of Levinasian ipseity is presaged in Kierkegaard's account of repetition and displayed in the temporalization of change in organisms that are described by some biologists as expressing "metastable equilibrium." More significant is the possibility for the "naturalization" of the Levinasian subject when his notion of self is seen as refracted through the lens of the autopoietic school of biology. According to its founders, Maturana and Varela, the observer who exists in and through language emerges as a result of the recursiveness of living systems. Self-consciousness is an outcome of the activity of the internal structures of unities that break through their isolation by means of language, relations that are seen as opening the way for a visionary ethics of love. In Levinas's account, the passive pre-originary self of ipseity is a living system, one for which not love but a preoriginary openness to the other who cannot be conceptualized is the condition of ethics.

Contributors

LEORA BATNITZKY teaches modern Jewish thought and philosophy of religion at Princeton University. She is the author of *Idolatry and Representation: The Philosophy of Franz Rosenzweig Reconsidered* [2000], and is currently completing a book on the philosophies of Emmanuel Levinas and Leo Strauss, tentatively entitled *Reason and Revelation: Levinas, Strauss, and the Possibility of Modern Rationalism.*

PHILIPPE CRIGNON is *agrégé* in philosophy and currently writing a doctoral thesis on *La figuration: Corps et politique de l'image* at the University of Paris VIII (Vincennes-Saint-Denis). He is a member of the research group "Arts, Appareils, et Diffusion" at the Maison des Sciences de l'Homme in Paris.

MATTHEW ESCOBAR recently completed his doctoral dissertation on André Gide at Princeton University.

LUCE IRIGARAY is Director of Research in Philosophy at the Centre national de la recherche scientifique in Paris. She is the author of many books, including *Speculum of the Other Woman* [1985], *This Sex Which Is Not One* [1985], *An Ethics of Sexual Difference* [1993], and *To Be Two* [2002].

ESTHER MARION is a Ph.D. candidate in French at Princeton University, writing her dissertation on Marguerite Duras.

SAMUEL MOYN teaches European intellectual history at Columbia University and is writing a book on Emmanuel Levinas's early development in the interplay of philosophy and religion in the interwar years.

PAUL RICOEUR is Professor Emeritus of Philosophy at the University of Paris X (Nanterre) and the University of Chicago. His many publi-

YFS 104, *Encounters with Levinas,* ed. Thomas Trezise, © 2004 by Yale University.

cations include *Freud and Philosophy* [1970], *The Conflict of Interpretations* [1974], *The Rule of Metaphor* [1977], and *Time and Narrative* [1984–1988].

NICOLE SIMEK is a Ph.D. candidate in French at Princeton University, writing her dissertation on Maryse Condé.

ALAIN TOUMAYAN teaches nineteenth- and twentieth-century French literature, literary criticism, and philosophy at the University of Notre Dame. He is the author of *La littérature et la hantise du mal: Lectures de Barbey d'Aurevilly, Huysmans et Baudelaire* [1987] and the editor of *Literary Generations* [1992]. He recently completed a book entitled *Encountering the Other: The Artwork and the Problem of Difference in Blanchot and Levinas* (forthcoming, Duquesne University Press).

THOMAS TREZISE teaches French literature, literary theory, and continental philosophy at Princeton University. His publications include *Into the Breach: Samuel Beckett and the Ends of Literature* [1990], as well as the French translation of Paul de Man's *Allegories of Reading* [1989] and the American edition and co-translation of Philippe Lacoue-Labarthe's *The Subject of Philosophy* [1993]. He is currently writing a book on Holocaust testimony.

EDITH WYSCHOGROD is the J. Newton Rayzor Professor of Philosophy emerita at Rice University. She writes on issues in continental philosophy of religion and is currently concerned with theories of altruism. Her books include *Emmanuel Levinas: The Problem of Ethical Metaphysics* [1974], *Spirit in Ashes: Hegel, Heidegger, and Man-Made Mass Death* [1985], *Saints and Postmodernism: Revisioning Moral Philosophy* [1990], and *An Ethics of Remembering: History, Heterology, and the Nameless Others* [1998].

ZAHI ZALLOUA recently completed his doctoral dissertation on Montaigne at Princeton University, and is currently Assistant Professor in the Department of Foreign Languages and Literatures at Whitman College. He has published articles on Montaigne, Diderot, Stendhal, Sartre, and Duras.

The following issues are available through **Yale University Press,** Customer Service Department, P.O. Box 209040, New Haven, CT 06520-9040. Tel. 1-800-405-1619.

ORDER FORM   **Yale University Press,** P.O. Box 209040, New Haven, CT 06520-9040
I would like to purchase the following individual issues:

_____

_____

MasterCard no. _____   Expiration date _____

VISA no. _____   Expiration date _____

Signature _____

SHIP TO _____

_____

_____

See the next page for ordering other back issues. Yale French Studies is also available through Xerox University Microfilms, 300 North Zeeb Road, Ann Arbor, MI 48106.

The following issues are still available through the **Yale French Studies Office,** P.O. Box 208251, New Haven, CT 06520-8251.

Add for postage & handling

Single issue, United States $3.00 (Priority Mail)   Each additional issue $1.25
Single issue, United States $1.80 (Third Class)   Each additional issue $ .50
Single issue, foreign countries $2.50 (Book Rate)   Each additional issue $1.50

YALE FRENCH STUDIES, P.O. Box 208251, New Haven, Connecticut 06520-8251
A check made payable to YFS is enclosed. Please send me the following issue(s):

Issue no.   Title   Price

_____

_____

                                               Postage & handling _____

                                                       Total _____

Name _____

Number/Street _____

City _____ State _____ Zip _____

- -

The following issues are now available through Periodicals Service Company, 11 Main Street, Germantown, N.Y. 12526, Phone: (518) 537-4700. Fax: (518) 537-5899.

36/37 Structuralism has been reprinted by Doubleday as an Anchor Book.
55/56 Literature and Psychoanalysis has been reprinted by Johns Hopkins University Press, and can
     be ordered through Customer Service, Johns Hopkins University Press, Baltimore, MD 21218.